the
GIVING
CODE

How charities can in*crease their* unrestricted income

Published by Whisper Books

Copyright © Rachel Collinson 2022

Rachel Collinson has asserted her right under the
Copyright, Designs and Patents Act, 1988, to be identified
as the author of this work.

Paperback ISBN: 978-1-7393697-0-5
eBook ISBN: 978-1-7393697-1-2

Cover design and typeset by SpiffingCovers

the
GIVING
CODE

How charities can increase their unrestricted income

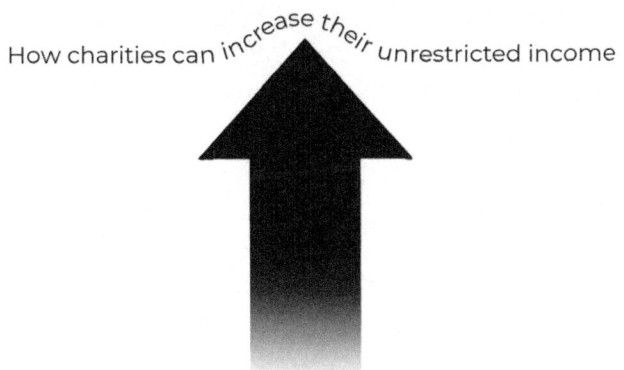

RACHEL
COLLINSON

To all those courageous people who give of themselves - and their own resources - to make the world a better place: minute by minute, penny by penny.

You know who you are.

'If you ever get close to a human, and human behaviour, you had better be ready to get confused.'

-   Björk Guðmundsdóttir

Contents

Introduction

Before we start...

When I talk about donors, I mean people who give time as well as money. This word, donor, can be someone who:

- Advocates for your cause
- Makes gifts in-kind;
- Volunteers;
- Campaigns;
- Organises;
- Leaves a gift in their will;
- Becomes a member;
- Fundraises;
- Writes encouraging letters to your staff or beneficiaries;
- Talks about your cause to friends and colleagues;
- Hosts events;

and in many other ways too.

Therefore, when I talk about a 'donation', this could mean a signature, an hour of pro bono counselling, or a crate of medical supplies.

And when I talk about 'fundraising', I mean anything you do that encourages people to give, whether time or money.

These other ways of giving are just as important as hard cash. People who give money also give in other ways. And all these other 'gifts' will ultimately save you time and money.

Aww shucks…

Blowing my own trumpet does not come naturally. So, when I describe success stories, it is because I want you to benefit from them. Everything in this book is based on solid evidence. Where possible, I have included quotes from my clients, or hard data.

However, I will also be open and honest about my failings. I am British after all. Sorry! Like my fellow tea-obsessives, I came out of the womb with a self-deprecating sense of humour. (Apologies to US readers in advance – I really do, gently, kick ass).

Enough apologising; let's get started.

How to read this book

This is a book for the change-makers of this world. Ironically, change-makers can become damagingly set in their ways. My deepest desire is that this book will help you knock your not-for-profit out of whatever rut it is set in. This is, I hope, the ultimate 'physician heal thyself' handbook.

Every charity is unique and every success, or failure story is unique. However, over the last 20 years I have noticed the same mistakes being made by not-for-profits everywhere, from the tiniest 'one man/woman show' to the highest profile international charities.

My mission in this book (which will in no ways self-destruct) is to guide you, to avoid the classic pitfalls, and also, learn the classic 'fixes' to your fundraising, that, again, work across the board.

Take a look at the following graph:

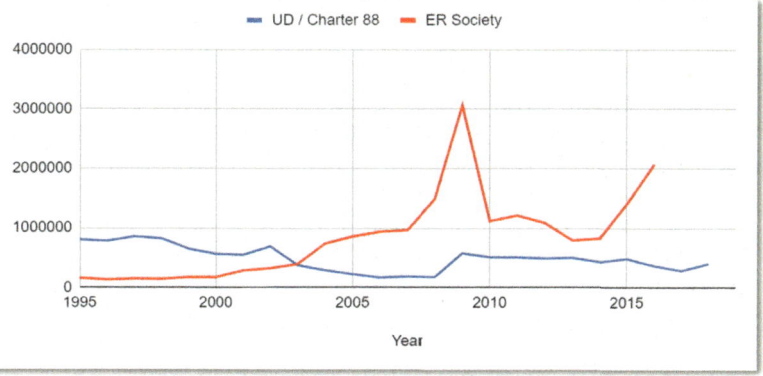

It shows annual income, in pounds, of two organisations. Two organisations that started in the same year with similar goals.

I know both non-profits, and I can tell you what made the difference between Team Red's rollercoaster growth, and Team Blue's sad whimpering decline. (Thankfully, Team Blue have started working with me in earnest and the situation has improved considerably.)

More on that later.

Better the devil you know?

For 13 years, I ran a web agency that served the third sector (charities, NGOs and social enterprises). Yep, all the do-gooders and so many good intentions.

The harder I worked with many of them, the stronger this nagging feeling became that something was awry.

We had an innovative, thorough process that we used to work with each client to build a new website. We got great feedback. We won awards and got interviews in design magazines. People referenced our work in books and academic papers. And the same clients would come back to us time and again with new projects.

This was of course a sign of good health. But something gnawed at me.

These organisations were paying me their donors' money— sometimes six-figure sums—to reinvent the wheel on multiple occasions. This struck me as poor value for money.

However, these were the clients. So we kept building new shiny things for them, even though it was, in essence, the same process each time.

Finally I sold my agency in 2013 and became a consultant. I had a burning desire to fix all the issues I had seen recurring throughout the previous 13 years. The non-profits I worked with were great, but they were used to doing things 'the way they have always been done'. I had become convinced that by playing safe in this way, they were missing a much bigger prize.

I believe that if there is a chance that a new and different method can make people's lives better, I need to try it. Sometimes that method fails. But sometimes there are new ways of working that work ten times better.

So, I want to help you benefit from all my previous trials, errors and successes. I have spent upwards of £80,000 of my own time and cash to explore new ways to help charities like yours grow their unrestricted income.

This book then, is the sum of what I have learned. It means that don't have to make any of those many and varied mistakes yourself, or indeed spend £80,000 of supporters' money doing so. You're welcome!

OK, strap in - what to expect from this book

I have structured the book as follows:

First, I want to help you paint an honest picture of the current state of your non-profit. If you are clear about this, it will be much easier to know which step (of the steps covered in this book) you need to take first.

As you read, you will encounter quizzes, designed to help you know how to proceed. Please don't skip these. They are essential if you want to get the most from this book.

In the next section, I make a case for 'values-driven fundraising'. This is a method I have created which will help you get the maximum unrestricted income from the smallest possible amount of time, money, and effort. This will leave you more money to pay your staff what they are worth and help more of the people (or donkeys…) your non-profit exists to serve.

You may have heard the phrase 'Hurt people hurt people'. Angry, hurting, resentful people can so often cause pain and hurt to others.

However, the converse is also true: 'delighted people delight people'. I want you and your staff to experience delight every day. And the only way to do it is to get more unrestricted income.

Money buys time. Time to breathe. Time to take care of yourself and your staff. Time to recharge. Time to ponder better solutions to problems. Time to grow.

To buy that time, you need that precious unrestricted income. To do that, we will look at the new choices you can make. These will set you up to reach new and even more generous donors

-donors who will trust you to use their money to make life better.

Next, I will share with you all the steps and strategies of my 'Values-Driven Fundraising System'. Each client who has followed all the steps in this system has seen their individual giving grow. They have grown, on average, by 202.8% after their first full year of implementing the system. No, I am **not** making that up!

Look, it's simple...

The message of this book can be summed up in four points:

1. Get to know your donors' values and motivations.
2. Test these at a scale that makes your conclusions reliable. (That's science!)
3. Create an 'irresistible lure' to draw in more of these same sorts of people.
4. Build 'forever loyalty' with a personal relationship of trust.

My goal is for you to have all the simple steps you can take for your non-profit, laid out, ready to start growing your income almost straight away. By the time you have finished this book, you may well have tried one or two of the ideas in it and seen your income grow.

Along with the 'Values driven fundraising system', this book is full of helpful anecdotes, tips and nuggets of wisdom that I have picked up over the last 24 years.

Yes, this is a fundraising book, but it attempts to go much deeper than that. This is about designing a better non-profit; one that has a deep and lasting impact. One that doesn't burn supporters or employees out along the way. I want your non-profit be a 'joy-bringer', uplifting everybody it comes into contact with. That is what every charity should be like.

And finally…

If you read this book and decide you would appreciate a helping hand putting what you have learned into practice, please apply for some time with me and my team here:

http://whisper.ist/breakthrough

Please note: our time does tend to get booked up quickly, so if this week is full, try another week.

Helping people like you do more good is what gets me up in the morning. It's nearly everything my team think about, every waking hour.

We are here to help you.

Here's to a better world!

Rachel Collinson

Part 1:
Stop trying to spin so many plates

Chapter 1:
What Your Future Could Look Like

Once you've cracked the Giving Code, you'll never again have to:

- See another staff member leave because they were struggling to make ends meet and your trustees wouldn't sign off the extra pay rise;
- Crank up the guilt factor and pester people with fundraising appeal after fundraising appeal, piling on the emotional blackmail to squeeze out every last penny;
- Watch your list supporter shrink, month on month;
- Fix the leaking sink yourself because you can't afford to get a specialist in to do it;
- Struggle to sleep at night, wondering how you're going to meet payroll;
- Shake your head at the mystery of your email list, not knowing who those people are, and why they don't respond to your heart-felt campaigns;
- Read emails that complain about being asked for money;
- Get that sinking feeling when you present the annual report to the board;
- See people cancel their planned giving because you pestered them too much;
- Sign off yet another burned-out worker on long-term sick leave because there's too much to do and not enough hands on deck;
- Spend 12-hour days doing the things an office assistant should be doing for you.

Instead, you'll be able to:

- Keep your staff happy by paying them what they are really worth;
- Add to your team;
- Stop the burnout;
- Work a 9-to-5 and have free time to think, dream and plot about how you're going to serve more people (or narwhals) and make the world a better place;
- Sleep easier at night because the flow of cash into your bank account is assured;
- Plan based on a predictable and growing income;
- Stride confidently into board meetings with growth figures;
- Look at an inbox bulging with requests to help from people whose names you've never heard of;
- Know exactly who your donors are, what makes them tick, and where to find more of them to grow your unrestricted income whenever you need;
- Fall in love with change-making all over again.

Client Case Study: Build the South

Here's how this looks in practice:

Build the South approached me with a problem. Their list of donors was shrinking, and their email list of supporters was static at 17,639.

Most of their supporters were people who had made a purchase on a sister site, the Black Dollar. This sold fairtrade goods. The Black Dollar would ask customers if they wanted to make a small donation to Build the South. If their customer said yes, they joined the Build the South mailing list. As a result, Build the South knew next to nothing about these fresh donors.

They joined my 'Find your next generation of super-donors' programme so they could understand their donors better and work out how to find more of them.

Build the South staff used our brainstorm process for creating an 'irresistible lure'. Using this unique method, they came up with a 'Holiday Justice Countdown'.

This was so successful it now runs every year.

At the time of writing this, about 18 months later, their list has nearly doubled in size to 34,630. Their income from individual giving is up from $1,382,134 in 2019-20 to $2,380,343 in 2020-21.

'Everything's exploded since the team started working with you. We've gone from net loss of donors to net gain. We've recruited loads of new people and got lots of campaign actions.'

– Dana, Head of Communications, Build the South

Later, I will share with you the exact strategies and tactics we used to make this happen.

But for now, consider this:

When you uncover the values that your best donors share, it's straightforward to find more of those people and attract them to your work. And when you do, you barely need to ask them for money, because they love you and trust you. They want you to help them make change happen.

That's the power of the values-driven fundraising system.

You will have a sort of 'magic tap' out of which flows new donors. You can turn this tap on when you need to grow your unrestricted income and turn it off if you get overwhelmed. (Imagine being so successful that you need to stop your outreach because there are too many people!)

If you are managing this correctly, your staff will need to spend fewer than seven hours a week—between them—to maintain the flow of new donors.

In the pages of this book, I'll give you a complete rundown of what makes this system work and why. It's possible that this will be the turning point for the growth of your non-profit.

The only way to find out for sure is to read every single word. It should take you less than an afternoon to finish, but could be worth millions of pounds or volunteer hours.

So, if you're ready to recreate the same success for your cause, let's go!

*Throughout this book, the names of my clients have been redacted or changed to reduce the likelihood that readers will lift specific ideas wholesale. Simply producing a carbon copy of an existing success story dilutes the value for everybody and can harm our sector. However, for those wanting to work with me directly, I am happy to produce sufficient details of projects to verify the claims of success made.

Chapter 2:
Who this book is for

I don't know if you've ever taken a personality quiz thing called StrengthsFinder. (I just love personality tests—I know some people call them 'horoscopes for middle class people'. Do I sound bothered?)

Anyway, the StrengthsFinder quiz showed me that one of my leadership 'strengths' is *Input*. I love to take in facts and knowledge. I do it all the time. My husband and I tell each other a 'fact of the day'. Yesterday's fact, since you ask, was: did you know Binturongs (cat-bears) smell like buttered popcorn?

Art college taught me new ways of seeing and processing information in all its forms. I tend to observe patterns. I spend a lot of time thinking about what could change those.

One pattern I see recur in the world drives me—like the Dizzee Rascal song title—BONKERS.

The best way I can explain it is to tell you a story about a non-profit I encountered:

This small team of organisers were talented at getting income from institutional funders like foundations and trusts. They were able to attract £100,000s in grants for their neglected-yet-crucial mission.

The better they got at doing this, the more they grew. Two years ago, they managed to get a major grant for some high-profile coalition work. This meant they could increase their workforce by 50%. Their funders and board were keen to get maximum impact for minimum spend, so they decided it made sense to create a few paid internships.

At first, all was well. The board were excited, and the funders nodded approvingly. Together they created lots of new jobs! The new staff and interns were so passionate about the cause that they went way beyond the call of duty with their work. National press and broadcast coverage followed.

However, it was soon clear the director didn't have time to support a much bigger team working on a wider range of projects. This was made worse by the fact that many of the staff were at the start of their careers and needed coaching.

Sometimes she had to choose between a crisis meeting and a TV interview. She was working 12-hour days to keep everything moving forward.

Doing more fundraising was simply out of the question.

The result? The organisation's income growth suffered. The staff deserved a pay rise for all their hard graft but there was no extra money available.

Worse was to follow. One year later, this small non-profit had to cut all the jobs they had created. Senior staff resigned in protest. Their team is now smaller than it was before. And all of this was so stressful that the director left, too.

The problem with paying your staff what they are worth is that it can be tough to persuade funders to give extra just for that. It is hard to draw a line directly from extra wage expenses to the impact you have.

Small non-profits are caught in a dreadful bind. You can't grow your income because you don't have the staff. And you can't get more staff because you can't grow your unrestricted funds.

This is just one example of a damaging pattern that your non-profit can fall into. The more I saw patterns like this, the more urgency I felt to find ways to escape these unhelpful traps.

I have tested all sorts of different ideas, read piles of books, talked to experts across the world, observed non-profits in action, volunteered for diverse causes, visited developing countries, went to conferences, listened to podcasts, tested and then tested some more. Finally, I built everything I learned into what I call the Values-driven Fundraising System.

This is the hard-won result of my work with upwards of 300 non-profits, large and small, from Australia to Brussels and Costa Rica to Dharamshala.

I found out how your non-profit can:

- Grow your list of supporters with people who are raving fans of your cause;
- Understand their values and motivations for giving;
- Talk to them in such a way that they give even without being asked.

This will only work for you if you are willing leave your metaphorical ivory tower and get your hands dirty. In the successful non-profits I work with, their teams love to learn and they love to talk to the people who support them.

Take Stop Dirty Money for example. When they came to me, they were bringing in about £10,000 a year from a list of 8,000 people. They wanted to grow their unrestricted income and their individual giving. They had a small team of only three people and it felt like they were running fast just to stay still. All three of them had to do everything from changing the toilet paper to talking to the worlds' biggest media outlets.

We worked together to implement the Values-driven Fundraising System. Over the course of 3 months, they spent 7 hours a week making small, simple changes to their systems. A tweak here, a change of wording there.

They were keen to learn and did everything my team suggested down to a fine level of detail.

They went all-in; even going so far as to write their own Standard Operating Procedure for fundraising, based on everything they'd picked up from working with the Donor Whisperer. (We didn't ask them to do this, but it's a great idea!)

18 months later, their income from individual givers has grown seven-fold to over £100,000 a year. Between the first and second drafts of this book, their list grew in size from 15,000 to 36,000 people. They began getting surprise donations of £500 here and £250 there. They now have a pipeline of major donors who have started to give them 5-figure sums each year.

All this happened because they learned how to talk to their supporters in such a way people were excited about giving. Sometimes even without being asked.

They have since hired new staff members and are doing less toilet roll shopping and a lot more talking to law-makers.

Is the Values-Driven Fundraising System really for you?

Sometimes people hear about what's involved in raising huge amounts of unrestricted funds, and they think it's not for them. They may give one of the excuses further down this page.

If any of these ring bells with you, read further. I hope I can reassure you, because I strongly believe most non-profits can— and not only that—*need* to grow their unrestricted income.

I - 'I'm not good with technology'

I'll level with you: I wish my clients had a new donor for every time I've heard somebody tell me this. So many of my clients have full-blown computer anxiety[1] . However, by the time we've worked together they are full of confidence.

Sometimes this transformation takes less than an afternoon.

I've taken care to design a system that takes you step by step through nearly[2] everything I know.

Now, this process does involve using tech, yes. It also requires spending some time and some money. However, once you've learned it, you don't need to come back and learn it again.

Often the things I discover with my clients mean that they need to spend *less* time with tech, not more.

---

1   Personally, I think this is part of the gate-keeping that happens with powerful tools; those who know how to wield them want others to think such tools are too complex or tough to fathom. This keeps the world the way it is. But I know how often that turns out to be nonsense. I'm here to up-turn that old order of things which has created so many problems.

2   You probably don't need to know all about New Order's back catalogue and related facts; just some of the other random things I know.

One client of mine—an NGO who work on a rare disease—
wanted me to put together their monthly email newsletter. I
started by looking at the previous month's edition. I'll be honest
with you here; it filled me with dread. Yes, me, a certified geek-
girl, the Collinson family IT support line, who taught coding to
post-grad students.

It was designed like a posh magazine. There were several
columns of different text and images, a smart colour scheme,
pull-out quotes, different stories and a message from the CEO.

I put together that month's version. It took me a whole day of
coding and swearing at my laptop.

I knew this was too much work for too little gain. I went to
them and said, 'Hey, can we test something different on a small
portion of your list?' Thankfully by this point they trusted me
and said, 'Of course, if you think it will get us more donations'. I
smiled to myself because they had no idea what was about to
happen.

I set up something called a split test. (Bonus points if you
already know what this is! It's a key part of the Values-driven
Fundraising System. You'll learn more about split tests later.) This
would send their old style newsletter (the one I'd slaved over
between bouts of bad temper) to most recipients on their list.

Then, I created three separate emails with hardly any design.
Just the client's logo at the top, plain text, a few photos here and
there. Each of those emails featured a single article or letter from
that month's newsletter.

That set of plainer, more personal missives took about two
hours in total to build. Piece of (vegan) cake. I sent one of those
emails each week to the smaller, remaining segment of the list.
(The randomly selected, unknowing guinea pigs.)

The result was jaw-dropping, even for me.

The three-email series—the one with each homespun-looking email focused on a single subject—**raised twice as much money**.

Twice as much money, for one quarter of the work.

If there's one thing I recommend you do, having read this far, it's that you follow this same advice. Stop sending out monthly, multi-subject newsletters to your list. Send one single topic email a week instead.

It doesn't matter if the design would make your graphic designer niece cringe or roll her eyes. It just needs to look like an email you would send to a friend. You know; the sort of email you actually want to open.

Clients raise thousands of extra dollars each year just from that one change. So, if you want a simple way to put my advice to the test, try running a split test in the same way I described earlier. There is a prize if you can record your results and share them with me. (Yes, genuinely! I read and reply to every single one of my emails.) Contact me via my website: www. donorwhisperer.co.uk.

All the steps I've outlined here are designed so a team of three can work on them together, to share the load.

One person might take on the bits where you need to talk to people. Another might take on the techy stuff like split-testing. Still another might be charged with recording all learnings and sharing them with others in your organisation.

You can make sure whoever is more confident in a particular skill set can do the lion's share of that work.

The Values-driven Fundraising System is designed to be simple and repeatable. It's not easy (I will admit putting it into action requires hard work, even if only to start with) but it is simple.

To show you what I mean, I want to tell you a little story that starts with Henry Ford's first assembly line in Highland Park, Michigan. (Shout out to Mark Stringer, agile development coach, who was first to enthrall me with this story.)

You may have seen those 1930s Pathé Newsreels where the plummy voice fawns over Ford's modern mass production method as begun in this factory.

The ones that showed rows of cars, each moving down the line, each made in the same way. Ford was said to be creating cheap, flawless machines, within reach of any family's budget. That's the picture I get when I think of Ford.

But that's not quite how it was in real life.

We cross the Pacific to Japan. It's the late 1940s, and an engineer called Taiichi Ohno is looking to improve the way cars are made. (That surname really does belie his talent; I think Ohyes would have been more apt.)

Ohno has heard about Ford's factory because of the impressive output. He decides to visit Michigan to see for himself how it works. But during the trip he observes that—although the company loves to boast about their process—it's chock full of errors.

So much so, by the time the cars roll off the line, a team of mechanics has to tinker for hours on each one, fixing all the problems. This creates a bottleneck.

The stock response to this kind of thing (from the 'Big Bank School of Toxic Business as Usual' at least) is 'Heads must roll!'.

Instead, Ohno pinpoints Ford's assembly line **system** as the source of most issues.

Back in Japan, he lays out a new business theory—almost a manifesto. From this point, savvy leaders know to look at production systems first, not humans, to root out issues.

Ohno's colleague, Shigeo Shingo (also a genius) is inspired by this new, more humane leadership.

Shingo starts to invent these clever widgets for building cars. Each one is designed so a worker, at any stage, cannot make a mistake.

For example, Shingo makes a device that switches a light on when a part is in the right place. His sockets are shaped so you can only fit the correct plug in each one.

This, he calls the 'poka yoke' system. In English, it's like the phrase 'mistake-proof'.

This data cable is an example of poka-yoke; you cannot connect it to its socket the wrong way. And there's only one sort of socket it fits in.

If even one small thing goes wrong anywhere in Shingo's factory, any worker can sound the alarm, and the whole system stops. Every single team member works on fixing the issue until it is sorted. Only then can the machines hum back into life.

All this is why Toyota—the company both these men worked for—is now the biggest car-maker in the world.

This is one of our values here at The Donor Whisperer. We look at the system first, before the person, to see what went wrong. It's why we work hard, and smart, to invent simple systems you can repeat, without screwing up.

Through these systems, you learn what works and how to avoid messing up for yourself. An organisation should not have to constantly rely on an outside agency for such wisdom. Instead, you need a functioning system that generates answers for you, directly.

This, in the end, makes failure hard.

It means that you can hire people for their character and values over knowledge and experience. This makes for a happier team who are more likely to bring the change you want to see in the world.

Here's to ~~smashing~~ fixing the system!

II - 'I don't like asking for money or help'

I wish my clients had a new donor for every time I've heard this.

If you have this problem, you are not alone! (Although it is strange how many people start or run non-profits who don't like asking for money or help. It's like meeting a farmer who's allergic to soil.)

But also, consider this.

While I write this chapter, I'm going through some intense pain (emotional and physical). I want to use this moment to remind you, and me, that we have the best job in the world.

Yes, really… we both have the best job in the world.

Jeff Brooks, master fundraiser, puts it better than I could:

'I know fundraisers [and activists]* who are almost ashamed of their work. They equate it with begging or even scamming, as if they're getting the better of donors in some barely tolerable way. As if their only defence is the sad argument that the end justifies the means.

'Anyone who feels that way simply isn't paying attention to what donors get in the deal.

'If you want to change the world in a meaningful way, I can't think of a better way to start than getting people to care with an act of charity as the first step. Donors are more kind, compassionate and active than non-donors. When you ask them to give, you support their habit of virtue.'

(This is from the rousing final chapter in his book 'The Fundraiser's Guide to Irresistible Communications'. I commend it to you.)

I learned this week that the act of giving stimulates dopamine in the brain. That's the same chemical that's released when you have sex or eat. It is the chemical that gives you that warm glowy feeling in your tummy (and I'm not talking about Cadbury's Options here).

Scientists tell us that your organisation's requests for money or time are triggers for that kind of pleasure.

By staying silent when you could ask for money, you cheat people out of that dopamine hit. More than that; deeper, more impactful: you are cheating people of the opportunity to satisfy their deepest desires: to do good in the world.

There's something else I need to point out here. There is a huge myth that exists in the non-profit sector around competition for donations.

The very week I write this, the Director of Comms at a well-known charity told me if other similar causes are asking for money, 'it means that we can't ask people for money'. I hear this most often from umbrella organisations. If that sounds you, I hear you. I see the important work you're doing and how hard it seems. But there is hope!

Let's say you are a sanitation charity, like WaterAid. Right now Oxfam are doing a big water appeal. You think, with good reason: 'Well, let's hold off doing our appeal because Oxfam are doing theirs.'

Some fundraisers think if people give to Oxfam's water appeal, they won't give to WaterAid. But the research tells us something else.

You are not competing with similar causes. Actually, you are competing with Starbucks and Netflix and Deliveroo and Amazon.

Most people don't have one household budget line for giving money to charity. Most people[3] don't have any budgets, full stop. They just look at their bank balance, and if they get a good feeling about that figure, they'll give a bit of it to you.

---

3   (Unless they're odd like me and they have a budget for giving to people and causes. But I'm pretty atypical on most things, to be honest.)

Even then, if someone stirs my emotions well enough, I will break into another budget to give (only fine cheeses and cake budgets are fenced off). And I suspect that if you manage to move people like that, they will often 'find the money' to give.

III - 'We don't have the money to invest'

I wish my clients had a new donor for every time... oh, you get the idea.

I'm afraid I have bad news for you: fundraising needs investment. You either spend money on it or you spend time. There is no magic wand.

Well—that's not quite true. Very occasionally lightning strikes, or the heavens open from nowhere. However, that means there are also droughts.

Rather than waiting out there in the storm, waving a fishing rod around (I mean, come on, that's just dangerous) what you need is a 'money gumball machine'. (All credit to Perry Marshall, digital marketing sage, for this lovely visual metaphor.)

Let's say you visit a magical fairground. There at the foot of the carousel is a row of devices that look like this:

Photo credit, Pete Alexopoulos

Your kid wants some bubblegum, so you pop in a pound coin. The machine clanks, you see all the plastic balls shift in their round sphere, and you hear a 'ka-chunk' that one has been dispensed.

You lift up the little metal flap at the bottom of the machine and reach into the small metal chute for the plastic bubble. You open it—and there's a two pound coin inside.

Wait, what? Must be a mistake, right?

But just in case, you fumble for your purse and put in another pound. Out pops another plastic bubble. You open it—another two pound coin inside.

Oh, boy.

You do the same again—same result.

I don't know about you, but my next move (aside from soothing a furious toddler) would be to run to the bank and change £1,000 into pound coins. Then I would rig up a giant chute to guide all that cash into the slots of those money gumball machines.

That's what investing wisely in your fundraising is like.

It might take a little while to find the money gumball machine, to change your notes into coins, and get your cash funnel rigged up. But once you're done, you can keep turning £1 into £2, and £2 into £10, and £10 into £50, and £50 into £250.

Exciting, isn't it?

If you are beginning to think 'but I can't even spare that pound yet' there's another little-known but crucial fact I need you to consider.

Most non-profits have reserves. Some people assume reserves are to pay your staff for three months in the event of an emergency. But there is so much more to reserves than that. If you don't know about the other purposes of reserves, you are doing your donors— and all the people or sloths you haven't been able to help yet—a grave disservice.

Reserves are there to invest in your growth as well as for use in an emergency.

How else are you supposed to attract new donors? Put the lightning conductor fishing rod down —you honestly don't need to invest that much time and money to start seeing your unrestricted income start shooting up.

Oh, and it is fun.

Speaking of fun, have you ever seen Taskmaster? It's a comedy show that kept me going through the pandemic lockdown. Regular 'crying with laughter' stuff. If you haven't seen episode 6 of series 11, 'Absolute Casserole' stop everything and watch. I hope you like madcap humour.

Anyway, I do believe it puts across rather well the power of tiny things.

On that note (and you might want to put down your coffee or your bagel before reading further) I have a story to further illustrate this point.

We rely on the historian Herodotus for the outline of this strange moment in time. He tells us that in the 6th century BC, King Apries of Egypt was worried his troops were about to rebel.

The King sent one of his generals, Amasis, to put a stop to it. The army's response? They crowned Amasis the new monarch of Egypt.

Whoopsie.

Meanwhile, Apries decided a subtle change of tack was needed, and sent over his advisor Patarbemis to speak to the General and all the troops he was now leading in mutiny.

Having heard the King's message from Patarbemis, Amasis lifted his robes, exposed his bottom and produced a single fart. 'Carry that back to Apries', he said.

Herodotus doesn't tell us how the poor hapless messenger relayed this to the King of Egypt. But we do know Apries responded in his usual thoughtful manner by cutting off Patarbemis' ears and nose.

When the Egyptian masses heard about this, they knew it was time for some regime change. A raging mob of thousands stormed the palace and tore Apries apart.

Thus began the reign of King Amasis in 569 BC, triggered by a waft of flatus.

In short: open the windows! Tiny actions can have huge effects.

As an example, one of my clients gained 50 new regular donors after a small change to their email programme.

Just one sentence, in fact.

That little tweak was worth over $11,600. Not bad for 20 minutes' work.

I know there are all sorts of mini changes you could also make to your digital fundraising or online advocacy. The kind that could give your work a growth spurt, right now. Much of my time is spent hunting for those tiny levers to push that will trigger big changes. Fragrant big changes...

Read on to learn some of those fundraising kickstarts.

IV - 'The board will never agree to this'

This is another objection I sometimes hear that puts limits on the growth of non-profits.

While I only want to work with the bravest people, boards are not, in general, risk-taking folk. That's ok—there are all sorts of scary laws they have to contend with. In some countries, they could get fined or sent to prison if they misuse donors' funds.

I know this full well.

I don't mean I've been fined! Just that, at the time of writing I'm on the board of two non-profits. I've taken care to read up on all the rules that apply here in the UK, and there are quite a lot of them. (That's me, as usual, practising what I preach.)

However, there's a cautionary tale the other way round, too.

Have you heard of Kids' Company? If you haven't, don't worry—they were a short-lived non-profit (in UK terms at least). They had a flamboyant and charismatic founder, Camila Batmanghelidjh. If you've seen her, you would not forget the moment. Her personal dress style was 'explosion at a fabric factory'—in a good way (I mean I love it!).

Camila was an expert at charming deep-pocketed givers. She could put together funding bids that impressed politicians and grant-makers alike. She raised hundreds of millions of pounds for children from deprived areas, many of whom had been sexually abused. This was much-needed work.

The board of Kids' Company held the view that child poverty in the UK was severe and an urgent problem to solve. They had hundreds of neglected children flooding through their doors each week. They felt the only ethical thing to do was to spend all their money directly on the kids.

This became the undoing of Kids' Company. Different bodies, experts and regulators gave them warning after warning: without investing in their fundraising to create sustainable income streams, the charity would collapse.

Sadly these predictions came true, with Kids Company closing its doors in 2015. This left thousands of kids without youth clubs and money for food.

You'll be glad to hear the UK courts recently cleared Batmanghelidjh and her trustees of any criminal wrong-doing. However, I would never want to be involved in a court case to which thousands of pages of evidence were presented. They must all have had dozens of sleepless nights and worked hundreds of unpaid hours full of regret.

All of this could have been prevented if the board of Kids Company had invested even a little in their unrestricted income. If they had focused on values-driven fundraising. If they could have developed a long list of donors who were giving for more reasons than one strong personality.

This is a scary story, for sure, but your board doesn't have to work hard to protect themselves. You have the answer to this problem in your hands.

Why not buy them each a copy, or lend them this one? (I really don't mind—you can even send them the PDF or e-book it if you want. You can have a license to reproduce it, un-altered, in full, with my blessing.The most important thing is as many people as possible read this book.)

Finally: they may not like to hear this, but it's part of your board's job to fundraise. They need to make a choice: do it this way, or ask their wealthy friends to pony up.

There is no path towards growth where they avoid investing in fundraising.

V - 'I don't want to do poverty porn/dehumanise my beneficiaries/guilt people into giving'

If this is on your mind, well done. This is a wise thing to be concerned about.

I was only six at the time, but I can still remember the global fundraising events of 1984—Band Aid and Live Aid—in response to a shocking famine in Ethiopia. I suppose it was my first experience of fundraising.

Those events had a huge effect on me.

I'm sort of glad I didn't realise at the time what a patronising exercise this was. 'Do they know it's Christmas?' sang Bob Geldof. (Of course not, Bob, they're mostly Ethiopian Orthodox believers, who celebrate Christmas in January, not December.)

I do think Geldof was entirely sincere. (I doubt he'd have said, 'Give us your f&$*ing money' live on TV otherwise; at the time, the ever-so-polite BBC decided to censor him.)

He and Scottish pop star Midge Ure wrote a song that was designed to raise maximum amounts of money. The lyrics tugged on the heart-strings of people in developed nations with Protestant and Catholic backgrounds.

I mention this doomed campaign because it epitomises so much that is wrong with the way our sector has done fundraising. It relied on:

- Sending the message, however overtly or subtly, that we in developed nations are superior to those 'poor unfortunate mass of people in Africa';
- Using images of helpless naked children in their last moments of life, with distended bellies from prolonged famine, too weak to brush flies off their faces;
- A facile approach to solving problems of hunger;
- Heavy emotional pressure.

Most Generation Xers, like me (the ones who came after the Boomers; the ones nobody talks about) are scarred by this event. Even though it was well-intentioned. The images we saw were horrific, and we gave, but then… what happened?

There was an ominous hush. For months and years after, I don't remember hearing anything about whether people in Ethiopia had been rescued by their white saviours.

About ten years later, I learned that most of the money raised had gone to line the pockets of corrupt leaders and officials. I believe this was because it was raised in haste by a team who were all new to famine relief.

Thus, me (and many others like me) now have a cynical distaste for pictures of starving children in countries we've never visited. Don't judge me for that… at least not yet.

When I see those pictures, I think: "You're breaking my heart now and you're going to break it again when I discover my money's gone into a bottomless pit".

There is a way to do fundraising better than this. A way that doesn't rely on heavy emotional pressure. An approach that preserves the dignity of those who get the aid, even though they might be at their lowest point.

What I'm about to show you in this book is a way to tap into people's values. Their motivations for giving; which in effect are the same thing.

These values differ from person to person.

The founders of Band Aid had to rely on horrific guilt triggers: footage of starving kids, because they were using mass broadcast. They had no way of finding out the diverse values of people watching in their millions across the world.

Now, with the advent of the internet and digital technology, you do.

Not only can you be wiser about how to advance your cause, but you have better tools to do it. And you are reading this book, which puts you in the top 5% of fundraisers. By the time you've finished reading, you will be at the cutting edge of what's possible.

So what does all this mean?

If this is you, you need the values-driven fundraising system.

Come with me to Freetown

The best way to explain why this is important is to tell you a rollicking roller-coaster ride of a tale. There's a juicy lesson you can take from it about the mindset of your supporters.

A while back, I found myself on a long weekend trip to Sierra Leone, with a charity executive director, two multi-multi-millionaires and a financial advisor.

The year was 2008. We were all licking our wounds from the Great Recession.

I had just started working with Prakash, leader of the non-profit in question. He invited me along to a major donor "show and tell" trip. It seemed like a good moment for me to join this long-planned journey, to capture content for their website.

The flight sticks in my memory for all the wrong reasons. Imagine the bumpiest flight you've had, times five.

There were flashes of lightning and extreme drops. The pressure was so intense something burst in the overhead lockers and water gushed out. People started crying 'Jesus, save us!'

After an apology from the captain for flying through a thunderstorm, we landed safely a few hours later.

The drama continued, though, as we had to make the journey from Lungi airport (built on an island) to the mainland.

We took a Mi-8 helicopter bought from the Russian military in the 1970s:

I was excited—a ride in a chopper was on my bucket list, though admittedly not the final item…

As we waited for our luggage to be loaded, the CEO of the non-profit turned to me and said 'Did you know the entire football team of Togo was killed on this flight last year?'

You can imagine what this did to the little joy I had mustered up. Meanwhile, the two millionaires started making jealous jokes about each other's net worth. They finished by agreeing neither of them were rich men; it was the billionaires who deserved that title.

Then one of the pilots hopped over the back of his seat to do the safety drill. He reminded us about exits, seat belts, life jackets, top ups, whistles, you know the score. Then he finished with, 'Please be assured that our pilots are highly trained and are the safest pilots in Africa'. At which point laughter erupted from most of our fellow riders.

Finally, we had arrived in Freetown.

Our long weekend was full of visits to different projects. We met Barbara, from the Milton Margai School for the Blind:

(Apologies for the photo quality—it was still early days for digital photography. That's my story and I'm sticking to it.)

Barbara volunteered with the VSO (Voluntary Service Overseas) in 1992. They sent her to Sierra Leone, and she looked for a good place to work. When she heard the singing coming from this school, so melodic and vivacious, she knew this was the place for her.

In 1994, less than two years after her arrival, civil war broke out. The VSO pulled out and they advised her to leave too. But she decided to stay, raise her own funds, and face the bullets.

She had no weapons, and yet she braved a stand-off with the rebels who wanted to commandeer the school for their army. Due to her shocking courage, the troops left, perplexed.

I believe she is still teaching kids there, nearly 13 years after we met.

Another place has also stayed with me:

It's one of only two or three places you could go to in Sierra Leone in 2008 if you had mental health issues.

This place was so under-staffed and under-funded they had to chain patients to their beds, to stop people throwing themselves from the windows:

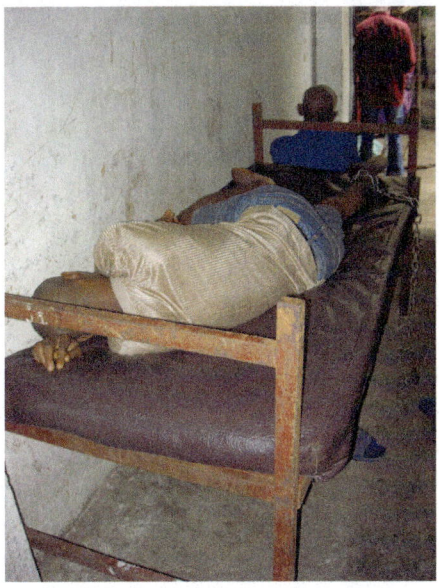

We also visited a disused abattoir. It was squatted by some men who had suffered the long-term effects of polio. It was the only safe place for them—elsewhere, contempt for disabled people led to vicious beatings.

Every day this man would drag his mattress outside. He poured sugar on it, to entice the bugs to crawl out of his bed, where he would pick them off.

Upon seeing all this, I was so overcome with emotion I nearly fainted and had to leave. Later on, I tried to record what I was feeling:

All through the trip, I wrote in my journal about the things I found most moving.

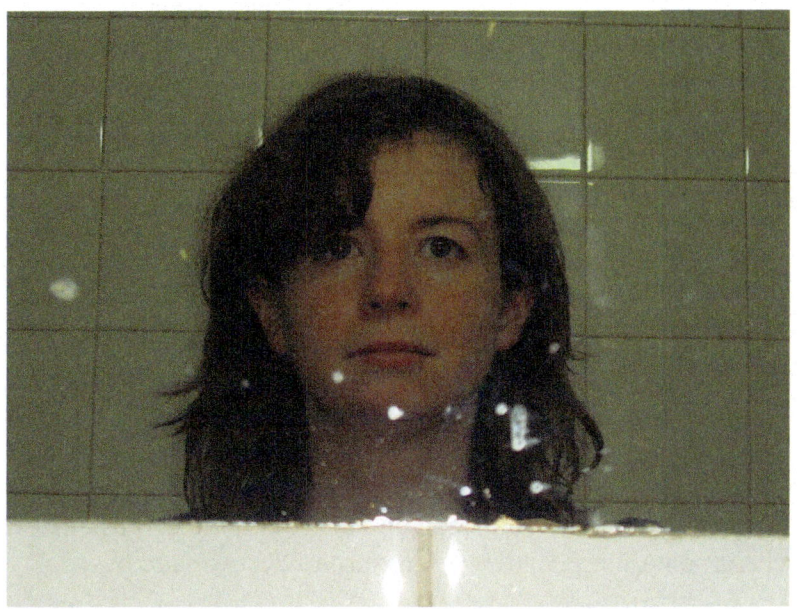

I couldn't stop thinking about the extreme measures people took to survive when they had nothing. Like the men and women suffering from mental ill health, shackled to their beds.

It felt like I barely had time to blink, and we were meeting for dinner on the final day.

Time for a debrief.

We sat in some wobbly white plastic garden chairs on our hotel terrace.

I asked the two rich guys what struck them most about all they had seen. They paused to think for a while. As they did, I wondered if they would mention the man with the proud smile who showed us an x-ray of the bullets still lodged in his back. Or a disabled woman who had built her own wheelchair out of old bikes.

After all I had seen, I was bewildered by their answer.

'It was Barbara', said Wei, the younger of the two. 'She is a legend'.

Barbara was the English lady who had volunteered with the VSO.

I was floored by this.

As we waited 8 hours in the airport for a delayed take-off, I mulled their words. I realised that feelings other than compassion may trigger people to open their wallets.

'Oh, you proper numpty', I said to myself. I had made the mistake of thinking that everyone feels and acts the same way as me. This is something I told my clients not to do, over and over.

This incident sparked in me a desire to learn all there is to know about the psychology of giving. One of the key things I have learned is that people's motivations for giving (whether money, time or social cachet) are based on their values.

Wei qi and Ming jie valued courage, risk-taking, and sacrifice. I valued equality.

Looking back, I feel sheepish about judging them, for holding different values to mine.

This then is the moral:

You must make it your mission to uncover the values of your donors. I can't stress too much how important it is to do this.

Once you understand your donors' values, you can speak directly to those values in the way you communicate. If you can trigger those values to create strong emotional resonance from your donors… well then, the sky really is the limit with your fundraising.

The Values-driven Fundraising System will help you uncover the values potential supporters hold, and thus what drives them to give.

This is a way of fundraising that goes with the flow of human nature. There is no arm-twisting. You can speak directly to the desires and motivations people already have. All of these come from their values.

When you offer a person the means to fulfil their desires, they don't need guilt trips or shocking pictures of people in dire need. They'll give to you out of hope and excitement.

Some 'experts' in this sector believe you must change people's values before they will give. I think that's making the same mistake as I had on my weird weekend in Sierra Leone. I assumed the values I hold (equality, social justice, benevolence) are superior to others' values, and they just need to be more like me.

That's the route to endless frustration and burn-out. You'll end up chasing people who can never be your super-donors.

I believe this is the reason our sector has made little progress in the past five to ten years on the world's most pressing crises. We expect people to care about the same things we do, for the same reasons.

Once you grasp this concept, you can achieve your mission sooner and with less struggle.

> ## Key Learning Points from this Chapter
>
> Knowing how to grow your unrestricted income is one of the most crucial things you can learn.
>
> Values-Driven Fundraising gives you the key to this. It is a way to understand the deepest desires and values of your best donors. Then when you show them how you fulfil those desires, they trust you to make good decisions about how to spend their money.
>
> Once you can talk the language of your best donors' values, you don't need to take people on guilt trips, twist their arms or use photos of beneficiaries stripped of their dignity.

Self-test: Is your non-profit in danger of buckling under the strain?

However, before you can fully benefit from this, we need to check in on where your non-profit is right now. I know everyone skips the 'exercises' at the end of chapters. In this case, please, don't, and please *be honest*!

Using this table, rate your non-profit on a scale from 1-5 on how accurate the statements are. One means 'No. Nope, not at all', and five means 'That is uncannily accurate – have you been spying on us?'.

Once you've put an X in each box that corresponds with your rating, total them up. Then use the Answer Key to see what the next steps are for you and your team.

There is an online version of this self-test here, if you want a robot to do the arithmetic:

http://whisper.ist/gcb-test-1

Statement	1	2	3	4	5
1. More than 80% of the work our directors or senior leadership team do is strategic in nature.					
2. I am able to delegate basic admin tasks to others.					
3. None of us have an issue with burnout.					
4. There is a low turnover of staff in my organisation.					
5. Staff are satisfied with their pay levels.					
6. We are able to provide good benefits to staff.					
7. I feel like there is a clear path to fulfilling our mission.					
8. It's rare that I have to work on weekends or on planned rest days.					
9. We are able to offer permanent positions to staff rather than temporary contracts for over 90% of our roles.					
10. I work no more than 7 hours a day for this organisation.					
11. I am able to take paid leave without feeling guilty about it.					
12. I love working on or for this organisation.					
Tot up your scores for each column:					
Grand total:					

What your score really means

Score: 12-36
Your foundations are trembling

I have good news and bad news.

Let's start with the bad news, which probably isn't news at all, least of all to you. Your non-profit lacks core elements required for long-term growth and staying power.

This concern may well be like an evil woodpecker whose beak drills away at you every day. It may manifest as a chronic health condition that resists treatment. Or you may feel a general sense of anxiety, anger or frustration.

The good news is all of this can be fixed. Even better, it means you get to rebuild those wibbly-wobbly foundations. If you and your team are able to do that with your own bare hands, you can be confident, because then you will know just how solid a foundation your organisation rests on.

If this is you, read this book with an open mind. Given how stressful and taxing things are for you right now, it will not take much for you and your team to see major shifts for the better.

Score: 37-49
A simple method for sustainable income growth will make life much easier

If your score got you here, it means your fundraising skills are helping a lot. But there are still things going wrong. You may sometimes scramble to meet payroll or upgrade your buildings or your equipment. Perhaps staff are due a raise, but you can't meet that cost right now.

You may need to diversify your income to make sure your future is assured.

Make it your mission to understand the values of the individuals who give to you, and what makes them tick. Focus on inspiring long-term loyalty. This will help you to withstand any economic and political storms that may be on their way.

Get ready to reward your staff (and yourself) with pay increases and benefits, as you see a year-on-year uptick in your finances. And look forward to the joy of expanding your work without stressing when it's time to run payroll.

Score: 50-60
You need to figure out how to scale up!

Great work! You are doing so well. You can be proud of yourself and what your team has achieved. All you need now is to put some rocket boosters onto this engine.

For you, the biggest hurdle to overcome is reaching new audiences as quickly as possible.

Values-Driven Fundraising will show you how to get your amazing work in front of many more potential donors while retaining your existing fans.

All you need is a bit extra learning, an experiment here and there, and you will be be poised to grow beyond your wildest dreams.

Chapter 3:
How to escape the death spiral

I have worked with some of the biggest non-profits in the world. Oxfam, Save the Children, UNICEF, to name but a few. I was one of a handful of people who banded together to campaign against financial institutions taking advantage of 'the little guy' and managed to get over £100,000,000 worth of debt cancelled or reclaimed. Not only that, I risked jail to do so. I helped to build one of the first ever Facebook advocacy applications. I have been voted in the top 50 most influential people in fundraising.

All this to say:

After 23 years of peeking behind the curtains of all kinds of non-profits, I have learned a few things about the **big** common challenges. I suspect one or more of these will be all too familiar to you.

I will also share with you the best fixes I've tried and tested over the last quarter-century or so,

Here, then are the biggest hurdles I see most often and how to overcome them:

Big hurdle #1: Your campaigns keep falling flat

A member of staff at a well-known environmental campaign once asked me a question:

'Should we give our supporters an option to press a "I can't donate right now" button?'

I imagine this came up as a suggestion because at least one person had emailed them saying that very thing.

However, there's a problem with taking this at face value. When somebody tells you they can't donate right now, that could mean one of two things. Either:

1. I'm living hand-to-mouth, and would be choosing between this or feeding my children;
2. You haven't convinced me to give yet.

Very rarely is the problem number one. In fact, people in group number one are generous beyond their means in a way that brings tears to my eyes. The reverse is true, too; people who insist they can't afford to give are often sitting on tidy sums of money. (I hear that Warren Buffett's wife still cuts out savings coupons from the local newspaper.)

If the true problem is number one (even then—are you *sure*?) it is vital you give this person other ways to help. This is a donation in itself; a donation of time. Such an offer will include and value everyone. Otherwise, people will go away thinking only landed gentry matter to you. Would-be volunteers or activists will conclude that they can't make any difference because they have little money, and walk away from you.

If the problem is indeed number two, then you compound it by being coy about asking for money. That is, *unless* you put this person into an email or other sort of comms sequence designed to increase their willingness to give. Or a sequence that helps you learn about their reasons for not giving.

Once you've eliminated number one, the reasons your donors say 'please no' to an appeal will always be one of these:

- The means of giving is too risky or insecure.
- I don't trust this organisation.
- This doesn't fit with my values.
- I'm not sure the money I give will actually do something concrete, or I'm not convinced this way of doing things will result in the change I want to see.
- Something else is more pressing, or I am not moved enough.
- The weather is bad today (or some other reason for a Scrooge-like mood that is nothing to do with you).

People will rarely, if ever. spell out which of these 'whys' is the real reason. This is because if I pause to examine my real motives, it can cause 'cognitive dissonance'.

This occurs when there is a mismatch between your self-perception and a new piece of information that has come to light. Cognitive dissonance creates profound mental discomfort in us, and most people will do almost anything to avoid it.

Our brains prefer to twist our thoughts until they resemble comic balloon animals filled with the hot air of denial, rather than deal with cognitive dissonance.

Instead of admitting the belief 'I consider my shoe collection more important than an injured donkey', most people just use the mental shortcut 'I can't afford it'. Or they might moan you're 'pestering me for money all the time' even when you only ask them once every quarter.

They know this is effective in getting you to stop asking, so they can avoid feelings of discomfort. We all do it. I do it myself. It's part of being human.

So, if people tell you porkies about their motives—without even realising it themselves, how on earth can you find the real reasons your potential donors are not giving?

I expect you knew I was going to say this: you use the Values-driven Fundraising System.

I helped the Green Party of England and Wales implement the system for the European Parliament elections in 2019.

Early that year, Heather Mack from the south-west of England came to me with a problem. How could they make sure their vital message cut through with voters in rural areas?

Together we ran a series of tests to find out:

1. Which audiences in those areas were most favourably predisposed towards the Green message.
2. Which messages would resonate with them most when it came to voting.

We found the images and slogans that best summed up the party's message and appealed most to different groups of voters. Then, we scaled up our ads.

What happened next was astonishing, even to me.

The Green Party's vote total grew by 55%, gaining over 160,000 more voters than ever in their history, even in areas where they had never worked before. In all, we had reached over half a million people more than the previous election.

A sure sign of success was that a far bigger party, the Conservative Party, saw how well this message did. They recycled stole it for their national election-winning manifesto later that same year.

Fast forward 18 months.

Using the Values-driven Fundraising system had laid the groundwork for the Greens to be 14 single votes away from taking control of Bristol city council. (Bristol is the biggest city in the south-west of England). This, despite having **one twentieth** the income of their two biggest rivals.

Self-test: How well do you know the people who support you?

Let's pause for a moment and see where you're at right now with this. I mean—do you know who your donors and supporters are, and what makes them tick?

Using this table, rate yourself on a scale from 1-5 on how accurate the statements are. 1 means 'No. Nope, not at all', and 5 means 'That describes me to a tee'.

Once you've put an X in each box that corresponds with your rating, total them up. Then use the Answer Key to see what the next steps are for you and your team.

Again, you can do the test online:

http://whisper.ist/gcb-test-2

Statement	1	2	3	4	5
13. I often see or hear strangers talking excitedly about my non-profit and our mission.					
14. I can explain with confidence exactly what our top supporters' values are.					
15. I know which phrases and concepts are likely to alienate potential donors.					
16. At least one third of our income from individuals is unrestricted.					
17. Donors often give to us without even being asked.					
18. Our donor attrition rate (the number of donors who stop giving to us each year) is below 20%.					
19. I have total confidence we are using the right messaging with our current and potential donors.					
20. We need to do only a few hours' work per week to attract a flow of new supporters, day in, day out.					
21. I am able to show our board of trustees why we are using certain messaging with our donors.					
22. I love asking for money or volunteers because we get such a great response.					
Tot up your scores for each column:					
Grand total:					

What your score really means

Score: **10-25**
Your fundraising is in trouble

If you're in this place, I feel your pain. It may feel like you're scrabbling around in the dark. You pour your heart and soul into fundraising appeals, only to have people give a few pounds here, a few Euros there.

You may have thousands of people in your database, but hardly any interest; low open rates on your emails and even lower click-through rates to your appeals. Plus, the disheartening unsubscribes every time you ask for time or money.

You might be more excited about by the prospect of banging your head against your keyboard, than running the next membership or volunteer drive. You have such a great cause; why aren't people falling over themselves to help?!

The problem is you don't know your donors. Well, you might know when their birthdays are, or what areas they live in, but you don't know their *values*.

Values are at the heart of nearly every decision we make. This includes how we spend our money and time. Once you understand a person's values, you know what motivates them. That means you can design and write your appeals in a way that floats their boat.

Not only that, once you get to know your donors well, it becomes easier to find more people just like them. And that is when things really start to take off.

The Values-Driven Fundraising System will help you to crack the Giving Code and unveil the mystery of why people are not giving to you. Pay close attention to chapters 9 and 10.

Score: **26-50**
You know some tweaks need making, but where?

You've built a great foundation for your fundraising. However, there are still some mysteries. It feels like when your appeal succeeds, it's more out of luck than because you understand exactly what will press your donors' buttons. Or you've got into a rut, and your fundraising is doing ok but it just isn't growing.

Once you've understood the Values-Driven Fundraising System, you'll have a much better idea of exactly what's not working. But most importantly, you'll understand *why*. You'll feel much closer to your donors and more confident of success when your team put together appeals. You'll see your donor attrition rates fall and your unrestricted income start to grow again.

Big hurdle #2: You are overwhelmed

I am in awe of you and the work you do for your non-profit.

It was hard enough for me when I was the executive director of a web agency with seven staff. But that was easier, because I had something tangible to sell.

Your job is way harder. It's not like you create and install easy-to-use, slick websites and mobile apps. Your results are harder to quantify.

It's no wonder you feel overwhelmed sometimes (if not all the time). Not only do you have the challenge of running a small organisation with staff who need to deliver projects, you have the challenge of fundraising, and all the extra legal strictures that non-profits must contend with.

To focus on just one aspect of this; there are so many different types of fundraising, and so many different channels you can promote them on:

- Telephone
- Zoom
- Tiktok
- Facebook
- Twitter
- Direct mail
- YouTube
- Specialist magazines
- LinkedIn
- Email
- Instagram
- Google Grants / AdWords
- Local newspapers
- TV
- National newspapers
- Clubhouse
- Pinterest
- WhatsApp

I could go on. A list like this can look demoralising.

It's no wonder you feel harried, bewildered and ready to throw up your hands in despair.

You are not alone. Other non-profit leaders feel the same way - I know; I talk to them every day. I don't want to downplay how bad this can feel. However, I want to reassure you that you are far from alone in this struggle.

The way out: know where to focus your time

I am sure you hear a lot of people tell you that you need a three-year strategy, or a business plan, or something similar. Then you will know where to focus your time.

Now, this is controversial, but I wonder if it resonates with you: three-year strategies and business plans are a waste of time.

There, I said it.

Yup—this is one of those humdingers I see all the time—things like 'Our reserves policy is that we need to have three months of expenses in total'. Or 'You should be able to get to any page on a website within three clicks'. These are all things people believe without having any real evidence to back up the beliefs. If you will, they are old wives' tales without the old. Or the wives.

It reminds me of that story of the religious order from over a thousand years ago. They lived in a monastery in a remote location; just them and one pet cat, to keep the mice at bay.

Every Sunday they would perform a special service with complicated rituals. Their cat would take an interest, jump up on the altar, knock candles over and whatnot. Because of the fire risk, the monks decided they had no choice but to tie up the cat during this service. (It's not like they had animal transportation cages in those days.)

Years later, the mice problem had disappeared. The cat died at a ripe old age. The monks mourned her.

The weekend after, the monks were performing their special service. One of them said, 'Wait, we need to get a cat.' 'Why?' said another. 'We need to have a cat tied up to complete our ritual'.

This is how a lot of habits outlast their useful purpose.

Let me offer an example closer to home (unless you are fundraising to help your religious order, in which case, please bear in mind that the cat was a metaphor).

Paul B Brown is an author and contributor to Forbes magazine. In 2013 he wrote of a great idea he had for a book. He wanted to go to successful entrepreneurs and ask them for copies of their original business plan. He figured you could learn a lot of interesting stuff by analysing these plans.

There was one problem; most of the business plans were *way off-beam*. You could read them and not be able to recognise the company they became. People who wanted to start a chain of hair salons started selling hair care products instead. Companies who wanted to serve shoppers became experts in helping distributors. Hardware manufacturers ended up selling software, or vice versa.

As Mike Tyson once said: 'Everybody has a plan until you get punched in the face'. (Many thanks to Zaid Hassan for this quote and the no-three-year-plan philosophy, which I've taken to heart.)

The longer you spend writing a three-year plan, the longer you are not talking to donors or beneficiaries. You are out of the real world. You are not sniffing the air.

You need to be able to scan the horizon with your own eyes. While you're holed up in your office, fiddling with spreadsheets, a pandemic could will pop up out of nowhere and up-end everything.

Except next time, it might not be a pandemic. It could be a terrorist incident with global repercussions. Or a supervolcano eruption. Or a bank run.

I don't mean to be gloomy, but my point is too important for you to take lightly.

As the writer of the Lean Start-up (a revolutionary business book that has created hundreds of millionaires since its release) says, you need to GOOB. Get Out Of the Building.

The Values-driven Fundraising System guides your 'GOOBing', so you talk to the right people and ask as few questions as possible to get right to the heart of the matter.

By the time you're done, you'll know the answers to the only four questions you'll ever need to ask:

- Who are my super-donors?
- What message makes their heart sing?
- Where can I find more of them?
- How can I win their trust?

When you can answer these four questions, you'll have cracked the Giving Code. All distractions fall away. You can focus your time. And all that time you'd have spent on putting together a three-year plan, you can save for helping more kids, or tree shrews.

Read on to learn how you can discover what the answers to those questions are *for you*.

Self-test: How Strategic Are You?

Before we move on to look at how to do all this, let's take a breather. I want to check in on how you're doing when it comes to your organisation's ability to be strategic.

Using this table, rate yourself on a scale from 1-5 on how accurate the statements are. 1 means 'No. Nope, not at all.' And 5 means 'That is an exact description of us'.

Once you've put an X in each box that corresponds with your rating, total them up. Then use the Answer Key to see what the next steps are for you and your team.

Yet again, there is online version of this self-test here, if you'd much rather a robot did the arithmetic:

http://whisper.ist/gcb-test-3

Statement	1	2	3	4	5
23. We have a strategic vision of how to grow our unrestricted income.					
24. We know what approaches we are going to try over the next year.					
25. We can easily measure our progress towards growing our unrestricted income.					
26. Looking back, I can tell you how we have achieved any progress in growing our income from individual giving.					
27. I know which social media platforms and comms channels to use for the biggest return on investment of time or money.					
28. If I had to take unplanned leave, my colleagues would be able to carry on growing our list and acquiring more donors without me.					
29. I have a simple document on hand that outlines this strategic process that I can show to funders, trustees, or new staff.					
30. At any time, I know what aspect of my work to focus on that will bring us the greatest return on investment.					
31. We consistently double our money on donor acquisition campaigns.					
32. I am able to delegate fundraising tasks that are outside my job description, with peace of mind that others would know how to complete them successfully.					
Tot up your scores for each column:					
Grand total:					

What your score really means

Score: **10-29**
Prioritise your strategic development before you drown!

I can imagine you're exhausted and ready to give up right now.
You keep trying different things to raise money, and none of
them work. You wonder how on earth so many charities raise
millions of dollars when it feels so freaking hard.

You're overwhelmed with choice, and you're spinning too many
plates already. Perhaps you bought this book in a last-ditch
effort to 'try one more thing' before throwing in the towel.

Even if you think I'm being over-dramatic, if you got this score,
then your fundraising needs urgent help. If you carry on like
this, you're going to keep bumping along the bottom, with the
same stresses and strains, for years... if your non-profit is able to
survive that long. One big funder pulling out could be the thing
that takes you under.

I do not want that to happen to a good person like you—and
definitely not to a good cause like yours.

One of the things I'm *over the moon* about showing you is how
to fix this quickly. I've seen that happen for many clients and it
can happen for you too.

It needs a little time (to read this book), courage (to go in a
different direction) and dedication (to persist until it works,
which it will).

Commit to following all the steps in this book, and you'll be
pleased with the results. Things can only get better, and you'll
make giant strides in no time.

Score: **30-50**
Focus for even better results

Hello multi-tasker. It looks like you've developed a knack for juggling about twenty-three different things all at once.

The problem is you can't stay focussed on one activity to really see good enough results from it. This is common among small charities who have built their organisation from scratch through hard graft. If that's you, I salute you.

However, you don't always know which fundraising activities bring you the best return on investment. Some of them will get you 80% of your results, and some will bring you no results at all. But you can't tell which.

It's frustrating that your donors come across as half-hearted sometimes. Many of them give as a reluctant duty, or so it seems to you.

The reason your unrestricted income isn't on a continual upward trend is that you are not testing and tracking it properly. If you could do this, you could let go of the parts that aren't working and optimise the parts that are.

If you:

- Uncover your best donors' values and motivations
- Figure out the messages to send them that will build loyalty and compulsion to give
- Then you can crack the Giving Code.

Having done so, you can put down the 'busy work' and focus on the meaningful work.

The Values-Driven Fundraising System could be the one system that helps you to stop spinning your wheels and instead, start multiplying your impact. Even if you don't like what you read today, the fact remains: you need to get in touch with the deepest desires of your donors and focus on those.

Big hurdle #3: Your funders won't pay for (enough) overhead costs

Remember that non-profit I talked about in chapter two? This is the issue that caused them to lay off and subsequently lose over half of their workforce.

Don't get me wrong; some funders will pay for overhead costs. This includes a brilliant fund called the Joffe Trust who are one of the few I've come across who do this.

Even if your funder is willing to cover staff salaries, fundraising costs and so on, you may still be nervous about asking for money for them. They may dictate you spend no more than 10% of their grant on overheads.

And yet, that really is the bare minimum. It's unlikely to be enough to see your staff happy and well-rested.

It doesn't help that we've trained our donors to see low overheads as a measure of success. (That's another story, and a rant for another day.)

Funders being squeamish about investing in fundraising, in developing staff, in giving pay rises, is what kills off so many promising non-profits.

I'm hoping many funders and workers in grant-making organisations will read this book. I would love more of these heroes to see that, *in their (well-meaning) aim to spend as much money as possible on achieving short-term goals, they are frustrating all their long-term aims.*

If you're a non-profitnon-profit who gets most of your funding from grants, and you live hand-to-mouth, or you hang on from one tranche of funding to the next, disaster is around the corner. You need the capacity to invest in your long-term future.

I don't want funders to perpetuate this short-termism any longer.

So, until or unless your funders take a more progressive approach to the problem of overheads, what can you do?

Invest in growing unrestricted funds from individual donors. Reach them and speak to them in such a way they fall in love with you and your mission.

Once you've built trust with them, that is to say, they can rely on you to:

1. Do what you say you will;
2. Keep them updated with progress;
3. Share their values;

then the rest becomes a piece of cake. From this pool of people will come major donors, large legacies, even introductions to corporate partnerships.

Key Learning Points from this Chapter

Knowing how to grow your unrestricted income is one of the most crucial things you can learn.

Values-Driven Fundraising gives you the key to this. It is a way to understand the deepest desires and values of your best donors. Then when you show them how you fulfil those desires, they trust you to make good decisions about how to spend their money.

Once you can talk the language of your best donors' values, you don't need to take people on guilt trips, twist their arms or use photos of beneficiaries stripped of their dignity.

Self-test: How Sustainable is Your Non-profit's Income?

At this point, let's analyse how likely it is for your organisation to last well into the future and/or fulfil your mission as fast as you can.

Using this table, rate yourself on a scale from 1-5 on how accurate the statements are. 1 means 'No. Nope, not at all.' And 5 means 'That sounds just like us.'

Once you've put an X in each box that corresponds with your rating, total them up. Then use the Answer Key to see what the next steps are for you and your team.

Or take online version of this self-test here, if your mental maths is flaky and you want the scores added up for you:

http://whisper.ist/gcb-test-4

Statement	1	2	3	4	5
33. Less than half our income comes from institutional donors like corporations, trusts, and foundations.					
34. I feel confident about our ability to grow, year on year.					
35. I am comfortable with the level of reserves we have.					
36. There is a strong upward trend in our income growth from other sources than institutional donors.					
37. The number of people who give time or money to us, on a regular basis, is growing overall.					
38. I feel confident about presenting our annual report to the board because of the strong financial position we are in.					
39. Our database of supporters grows consistently, week in, week out.					
40. I know exactly how to get new donors when I need them.					
41. I have an unrestricted funding program that works well.					
42. Donors are happy to invest in our sustainability or trust us to decide how to use their money wisely.					
43. I can make reliable projections about our income from individual givers for the next 12 months.					
Tot up your scores for each column:					
Grand total:					

What your score really means

Score: **10-29**
Beware!

If you were the pilot of a plane, red lights would be blinking on your control panels everywhere. Mayday! Mayday! Your organisation is flying a dodgy 737 with no parachutes or top-up tube on your lifejackets.

Make it your priority to turn things around before it's too late. You need to get your income generation into a place where it creates lasting growth or pays for itself.

This book will show how you can crack the Giving Code and grow your unrestricted income. Carve out time to focus on it tomorrow. Your staff and your beneficiaries will thank you.

Score: **30-50**
Get ready to turn the corner

You are in a good position to grow your unrestricted income. You probably just lack the confidence to make bold moves.

What you need is a solid framework on which to base your fundraising investment decisions. Then you can move forward with courage.

Be prepared to see your income growth take off as you put into practice the cutting-edge strategies and tactics in this book.

Key Learning Points from this Chapter

- To stop your campaigns falling flat, you need to get to know the people who support you;
- You don't need a three-year plan to grow your fundraising. You need a process.
- If you want to secure the future of your non-profit, you can't rely on grant funding alone, as it limits your unrestricted income. To be able to breathe, you need to invest in growing your income from individual donors.

Chapter 4:
Why values-driven fundraising is key

Ever since that weird weekend I spent in Sierra Leone, I have been working on a mental puzzle.

Humans of all cultures, ages and countries keep giving time and money to benefit strangers or even a different species. Why?

If you were a biologist, at first glance you would think this makes no sense. Surely, if an animal gives of their own resources to another animal, that goes against the theory of evolution, because they don't share any genes. For decades, this has confounded scientists.

After over thirteen years of thinking, observing, reading, learning, theorising and testing, here's what I know so far:

Every potential donor needs to be able to affirm these four things (not out loud; that would be weird. But they need to be feeling it, even if it is not a conscious sentiment):

- I can see that this organisation share my values and offer me a way to contribute that fits with my habits or lifestyle.
- I am motivated to give them my contact details.
- I trust them to use my money, time, or other resources wisely.
- I can see how we have made a difference together.

In later chapters, we'll go much deeper into the theory of Global Human Values. This will give you a reliable, scientific grounding in how to develop messages that resonate with your potential donors. We'll also look at how to cement that initial interest with long-lasting trust.

For now, let's explore these four keys to the Giving Code. All of these need to be satisfied for your donor to commit to giving you precious funds on a planned basis.

1. This organisation share my values and offer me a way to contribute which fits with my habits.

Some non-profits here in the UK use what I call the 'spray and pray' method of fundraising. They put their message out to all and sundry, far and wide, with no thought to targeting. They then need to rely on heavy pressure to sign people up to give regularly.

The poor souls who are paid to go out and do this kind of fundraising, door-to-door, or on street corners, are so familiar to us Brits that they have attracted a derogatory name: chuggers. (This is a shortened version of 'charity muggers'.) Only don't call them that to their face; they really don't like it.

This seems to be effective in the short term. In fact, it's so effective that fundraising managers are willing to pay over £200 per donor they sign up in this way.

However, there is a lot wrong with this method of fundraising. You can see it in the frighteningly high attrition rate of donors who were signed up in the street. Around 50% of them will stop giving in their first year.

And will they ever go back? I doubt it.

The kind of tactics you need to use to persuade somebody to give, - despite the fact you have interrupted their lovely shopping trip, or dinner at home with their family - can leave a sour taste in anybody's mouth.

There is a way that is far superior for attracting people's interest.

For this, you need to understand the MoVA formula. (It's pronounced 'mover', if you have nothing better to discuss at dinner parties)

- **Mo**tivations
- **V**alues
- past **A**ctions/habits.

The best way of explaining how this works is to tell you what happened when some academics at the Universities of Connecticut and Westminster came to me for help. They wanted to carry out a big research study/experiment that would run over 21 days, worldwide. It aimed to test a handful of new inventions for improving online comments on news articles.

I'm sure you can agree the world needs more of this kind of study.

At the time the project was called Scholio, but we thought that sounded too much like a painful disease, so we renamed it WeDialogue.

The researchers needed to get thousands of volunteers to join the experiment and stay with it for three weeks. This was no small challenge.

So I used Values-Driven Fundraising to help them.

To start with, we made hypotheses about the kind of people who would volunteer for this trial; what their values were and what would motivate them.

On our first try at promoting the trial, we got truckloads of menacing, rude and horrible negative comments. The team were truly disturbed by some of them.

Despite that, I sat down and thought to myself, what are these comments really telling us?

I realised we had made the wrong assumptions about our audience's language; and especially their values. Using the phrase 'safe space', for example, marked us out as liberals. Because of this, a lot of people didn't trust us. And the liberals themselves were warned off by bigoted comments.

A large part of our audience clocked straight away that we were not from their 'tribe'. Many others thought it was a scam.

So, back we went to the drawing board.

Having analysed the comments to uncover the values of the people who most wanted to engage, I rewrote the messaging. I chose imagery, headlines and advert text that was much more likely to appeal to that audience. I was careful to use their language.

We put the emphasis on who was behind the project. We started to talk about scientific methods and imbued our messaging with values of discovery and learning.

We went from a few dozen volunteers (and an army of trolls on the warpath), to no trolls and 1,500 volunteers, in the remaining time.

As I type this, the weather in Scotland is balmy. If you're in a place like Minnesota where there's freezing rain or you're in Texas, suffering from the baking hot sun (or even if you're in Scotland most of the year) that may be hard for you to picture.

In Nairn, where I'm currently working, there's a slight breeze and the sea air has that fresh, ozone-y smell to it. I wish I could click my fingers and magically transport you here so you can take it all in.

Some of your supporters will wish that too: for you to feel what they feel.

Make sure to step into their world—not just once, but all the time. While you're there—slow down. Sniff the air. Look. Listen. Drink. Touch.

Just like a good tourist, when you see a supporter responding in weird ways, use empathetic curiosity. Resist the need to 'tell' or 'educate' them. Ask questions that allow them to tell their story. Keep going until you understand them.

This is a skill I teach my clients. When we go through this process together, we always find buried treasure.

Here's to empathy!

Let's look at the next thing that needs to click into place for your potential donor to give.

2. I am motivated to give them my contact details

There are two ways non-profits go wrong with this step.

The first one is to bore your potential donors to death. To make it seem like you aren't all that bothered whether people stay in touch with you.

For a little while I worked with an international NGO who are not well known outside their origin country. We were looking at how to improve their website.

One of the first things I dug into was the newsletter sign-up system. I wanted to find out how effective it was. So, I filled in the form.

Usually, when you do these things, you at least get an email straight back with a thank you message. But there was nothing.

'What happens to these sign-ups?' I asked them.

There was a pause and some nervous shuffling. I think a tumbleweed might even have rolled past.

'That's not supposed to be there', they said. 'We thought we'd taken it off all the pages on the site because people weren't signing up'.

If this had been on a Zoom call rather than in person, I'd have switched off my camera to perform a dramatic facepalm.

Aside from the fact that this was a huge, wasted opportunity, my client didn't seem to realise they just needed to give better incentives for people to sign up.

Traffic to your website is almost like 'free money'. You need to take advantage of it! But you must make it worth your donors' while. (Unless you are in luck and they are already raving fans by the time they find your website.)

The other way non-profits go wrong is to overshoot. To my shame, I was part of this, a long time ago.

Let me explain. An example of this comes from when I ran a web agency.

Web agencies, fundraising agencies, advertising agencies and other creative outfits are incentivised to create a 'black box' for you. What I mean is that you have a thing that works to bring you new donors, but its contents are mysterious. You don't know *how* it works or how they built it. If the agency folded, and you needed to build another one, you wouldn't know where to start.

This is not by choice. It's the only way their business model works; the only way they can keep the lights on and the kids fed. In general, agencies make small profits, if they make a profit at all.

Most of the people I know who run agencies are great people with good hearts. And their model works well for non-profits who want tens of thousands of new supporters quickly, and have the money for that but no staff time. Or non-profits who prefer their staff to focus on the core mission, and let outside organisations do the fundraising.

Other folks like me set up their agency because they love tech and they love designing fun stuff. But when they are successful and they grow, they hire staff, and that's when the trouble starts. They're under pressure to keep the sales coming in to keep those staff salaries paid.

The problem comes because agencies can't just switch their payroll off and on when charities decide they need a website. They must either become super-efficient or work on generating demand for new, shiny-shiny widgets and cool things.

My agency decided to generate demand for cool things. We became known as the go-to people for any non-profit who wanted a Facebook application. (This was back in the days when everybody was still throwing sheep at each other. Remember that? This is going to read strangely for anybody who can't remember that light-hearted time in the internet's history.)

A global non-profit, let's call them BlueHaven, came to us with an idea for an application that would collect names and email addresses of people interested in saving the planet. It was called 'You Turn the World'. The idea was you could overlay a photo of your face onto a 3D spinning globe.

I was concerned this wasn't going to be fun or interesting enough for BlueHaven activists to do. If I'm honest, there was also the temptation to make something super cool, a viral hit, that we could put in our portfolio of client work.

So, we suggested adding a game to it that we called 'Climate Consequences'. It was a bit like Mad Libs. The idea was to write a madcap story together with a friend about world leaders saving the planet. And there would be prizes for the best one.

I can't remember how much money BlueHaven spent on my team, but it was a lot. And unfortunately, the application did not work well at all.

Those who 'got it' and played with it had a lot of fun, but in the end they got mere hundreds of people signing up. This was much lower than the tens of thousands that BlueHaven wanted.

I was gutted.

That's the other thing you don't want to do, laid bare. You don't want to get overly fancy and complex before you know if people will like the concept and share it.

So, what can you do instead? You build a prototype of what I call an 'irresistible lure' as quickly as you can.

You use free or cheap tools to do this, or even tools you already have access to. Then you get it out there, you learn from the response, and you iterate.

Many people think you need to get the right idea first, and then build it perfectly and people will come. But the idea is less important than the process.

What is most important is that you have a process for testing and refining it at low cost before you hit on something that works. Only then would you invest more in polishing the design, refining the content, and scaling it up.

My team walk alongside our clients as they learn exactly how to do this, and we can also do it all for them.

Now let's look at the third thing donors need to feel before they'll give.

3. I trust them to use my money, time or other resources wisely

Facebook has done some good things for non-profits, but in a lot of ways, it has done us damage. I find this upsetting because if Facebook took time to understand the sector (in the same way it has done with fashion, or gadgets) it could do some real good.

One of the ways Facebook set you up for disappointment is that they encourage you to add a donate button to your Page. There's a lot of hoops you have to jump through to get it.

Some non-profits I know have spent 20 to 40 hours wrestling with support systems that rely on AI, automation, and workers with barely any training. Over and over, that system comes back with answers to a different question than my clients have asked.

The main issue, though, is what happens once you've gone through this process. (If you're still alive by that point and you have resisted the impulse to launch your laptop through the window in a rage.) Facebook leads you to believe that people will donate as soon as they see the donate button.

Alas, that's not true.

For large non-profits: household names, with a big, established brand, who have millions of supporters, like Oxfam or the NSPCC, this can work.

People will have heard the name of these big outfits, seen their work (and even its results) often enough, such that when they see the non-profit's logo, they recognise a brand they can trust.

Trust is one of the most important factors in giving.

Think about it. Your donor is giving their hard-earned money (or hard-won time) to you, and they don't expect anything in return other than a glow on the inside and other blissful feelings. They must trust you more than most brands to do that. It's not like they get a pair of trendy new sneakers in return for giving

Big brands have millions of pounds and thousands of staff in their team. This means it's much easier for them to maintain that trust.

Advertising experts say that a person needs to see a product or logo three times in at least three places before they feel secure enough to try it. Some say it's even more than that; up to twenty times. Either way, familiarity breeds trust.

This is how human beings have evolved—we don't tend to like new things. A new thing could kill you! Our brains are hard-wired to be fearful of unfamiliar stuff. This is why companies and big non-profits spend so much on advertising and promotion.

You, on the other hand, can't afford for your non-profit to be on billboards, t-shirts, TV programs, school education packs and all over the newspapers, all at the same time. And I don't really want you to afford that—it seems rather wasteful to me, when there's a better way.

What better way is that?

It is to think of wooing donors as you would think of dating (and I don't mean 'terrifying')

Imagine that this lovely donor has caught your eye. You know they share your values. It could be a beautiful, lifelong friendship. You want to win their heart. And they've already given you their number, hooked in by your 'irresistible lure'.

At this point some non-profits think: 'Right, they like us, so let's put a ring on it right now before they get away!'

Bit forward, isn't it? Most dates would get scared off by that.

What upsets me is that there are some organisations, and people, who take the view if their 'suitor' didn't say yes to this premature proposal then the poor soul they caught off-guard is therefore not 'the one'. 'Next!' says the non-profit, and they move on to another potential donor without looking back.

I sincerely *hope* I don't need to tell you how daft that is.

At least in Western European cultures, you don't ask a person to marry you on the first date. You take time to 'woo' them. Show them how charming and fun you are. How well you treat them and others. How good you are at listening. You go different places together and do life together.

Then, you test the water. Are they looking into your eyes and smiling? Are they asking you good questions? Are they laughing at your jokes?

If all those things line up, then you might make a move for a hug or a kiss. You might ask for another date.

Maybe four or five dates in, if things are still going well then you'd perhaps raise the subject of, as my Grandma used to call it, 'going steady'.

I might be labouring the extended metaphor here a bit (and showing how long I've been out of the dating game), but you get the idea. Asking for a person's credit card details the first time you've met them; that's waaaay too forward. Your donor needs to know, trust and like you first.

Before you can ask for a cash gift, or a few hours of time, you need to do some groundwork. You must get to the point where your potential donor not only trusts you but feels delighted by what you send them. Then they'll feel compelled to give to you.

Another huge mistake is to ask your donors for more than you give back to them.

I'm not talking about money here; I'm talking about delight, love, joy and more of the feel-good emotions we all crave.

Recently, I was struck by a comment a random person made on a non-profit's Facebook post:

'They just want to get your details so they can bombard you'.

A lot of online comments can be hard to read, but many can teach us something—if we have ears to hear.

What you might conclude from reading this one, is that you need to send fewer emails. But that's the wrong thing to infer. It's not about speaking less, it's about changing the *way* you speak.

I say this because of the precise language this person used.

The word 'bombard' suggests a kind of attack they want to hide from. I hear that; I get emails from non-profits that make me feel awful. I feel like I'm just a cash cow, or I'm only a worthy human being if I give money.

Even if you only send one guilt-inducing email a month, that would still come off as a barrage. Why? **You are demanding more than you give back.**

The way to avoid this mistake is to ensure that for every email you send that asks for something hard, like giving money, you send three emails with no ask or an easy ask.

To make that easier to understand, look at this as a ratio:

3:1

Three for each email with no ask (or a 'soft ask'), per one email with a request for time or money (a 'hard ask').

Here are some examples of no ask/easy ask emails:

- A 'behind the scenes' look at what your staff or fieldworkers do.
- A heartfelt thank you and admiration for them as a person.
- A virtual birthday card.
- An opinion poll.
- A short survey.
- Spotlight on a volunteer.
- Interesting facts about your cause.

- The story of your founder.
- A petition you would like them to sign.
- An endorsement from a patron.
- An inspiring story of somebody who left you a gift in their will.
- A change in policy that happened as a result of your work.
- A funny anecdote that relates to what you do or a member of the team.

When you think about it, there are so many things you can tell supporters about you, them, and the work you do together.

Our supporters need to feel loved and valued as the unique human beings they are. More than that, they are the heroes of your story! You are the Yoda to their Luke Skywalker.

Your supporters are not vending machines. They love to give, but only when they are cherished and supported in return.

Try sticking to this 3:1 ratio. When my clients make this change, they always come back to tell me they are deluged with lovely replies. And their income grows.

I'll talk in more detail about both these 'better ways' later in the book.

4. I can see how we have made a difference together

This is the final part of the Giving Code you need to have in place. When your donor thinks this, you have the potential to make a friend for life. Such a person may give to you for years, give bigger gifts and finally leave a lump sum to you in their will.

By the way, this isn't always a neat progression.

One of my clients was surprised out of the blue by a cheque for £10,000 from somebody who wasn't even on their database. This man had been watching them carefully for a long time without giving. He had compared them with other charities he was also thinking about funding with his life savings.

This principle still holds true, as he was studying what set them apart from other causes. This client had mastered the art of doggedly explaining the difference they made. They sent out good news stories with photos as proof, week in and week out.

Non-profits leave billions of dollars on the table when they forget to do this.

Some organisations get so caught up with putting together the perfect appeal, they neglect to update their donors on the good news that has come out of their work.

That is the whole point of giving. Doing this is like playing a game of soccer and forgetting to put the ball in the net.

I do get it: sometimes things don't go as you expect. You didn't raise as much as you hoped. You weren't able to fund the full education of the student, or your lobbying efforts failed. You feel sheepish about coming clean with your donors.

What you may not realise is that when you're honest about your failures, donors who love you may well respond by giving even more.

Charity: water are a case in point here. They excel at updating donors on what their money has done, which is the main reason they have been successful.

They started doing live broadcasts of water well drilling in remote villages. One beneficiary, the Bakaya people from Moale in the Central African Republic, had been waiting over 10 years for their water well. During previous years, other teams had struggled to find the right spot in the ground where there would be water.

Geologists hired by charity: water recommended they drill down to 700 feet. So, Scott, the founder, ordered equipment that would reach a depth of 800 feet.

They started the 'Live Drill', confident of success.

But things went very wrong, in full view of thousands of people watching live online. Not only was it embarrassing but it was also a moment full of despair and exhaustion for both workers and villagers. How tough to have that play out in public.

Scott could barely bring himself to think about the responses. What would people say?

But then the posts started to come in on social media, and they weren't what he expected.

This is what he said about it:

'Our staff was surprised to see the responses... were overwhelmingly positive and encouraging. We got Tweets saying, "We appreciate your transparency". We got Facebook comments that said, "I think this is perhaps even more important than sharing your successes". We even had a field engineer chip in: "Even with the best planning, scientific data and equipment, you can have a myriad of problems... thank you for sharing the challenges".'

As well as failures, there are successes. Every time you have one, no matter how small, or how life-changing, make sure to share it with your list **as soon as you can**. The same day is ideal. But especially with your donors, quick quick. (Or, as my Grandad used to say: 'in two shakes of a lamb's tail'. And those little floofs can shake their wee tails so fast they're a blur).

People give because they crave to express their values and satisfy their desires. Often, this works on an unconscious level.

Take the research of Nobel-prize winning scientist, Ivan Pavlov. He invented the famous dessert 'classical conditioning' experiments. If you've already heard about those, you can skip this bit.

Pavlov was fascinated by animal digestion. He noticed dogs would salivate before food was delivered to them. To him this seemed almost 'psychic'. He wanted to see how dogs could achieve such a feat.

He theorised that the animals' unconscious minds clocked changes around them that would occur before food arrived—and the saliva was a reflex.

For months, whenever Pavlov fed his dogs, he rang a bell. He repeated this over and over. Then, he tried ringing the bell outside of feeding time. The dogs would salivate spontaneously. This stimulus—which had absolutely nothing to do with the food—would still produce a reaction in the dogs, as if food was about to be provided.

Bell -> Food
Bell -> Food
Bell -> Food
Bell -> Salivate -> Food
Bell -> Salivate -> Food
Bell -> Salivate -> Food
Bell -> Salivate
Bell -> Salivate
Bell -> Salivate

This works on humans as well. Have you ever caught the smell of a perfume, and been instantly reminded of the person who wore it? Not only that, you can even relive your feelings about that person?

There's a particular brand of sunblock I love to smell. It transports me back to a perfect, carefree, romance-filled summer in my late teens.

Sorry, where was I?

Back to my point: like Pavlov's dogs, if you can set the following sequence in your communications:

See appeal -> Give -> Read how the gift made things better -> Feelings of joy and hope
See appeal -> Give -> Read how the gift made things better -> Feelings of joy and hope
See appeal -> Give -> Read how the gift made things better -> Feelings of joy and hope

Then this can happen:

See appeal -> Feelings of joy and hope
See appeal -> Feelings of joy and hope
See appeal -> Feelings of joy and hope

Now, of course this takes some while for the connection to be formed in a supporter. Let's say you establish the habit of making appeals for time or money, and you always follow up with donors a few weeks later to share the outcome of their giving. That's a healthy routine to set up for many other good reasons. Compulsive giving is 'just' a glorious side effect of the things that will grow your unrestricted income, volunteer hours or advocacy actions.

Key Learning Points from this Chapter

Before a person will give to you on an ongoing basis, they need to feel or affirm these four things:

- This organisation share my values and offer me a way to contribute that fits with my habits.
- I am motivated to give them my contact details.
- I trust them to use my money, time or other resources wisely.
- I can see how we have made a difference together.

Chapter 5:
The problem with growing mass individual giving

I love showing clients how to treble, quadruple or even multiply their unrestricted income tenfold, from mass giving.

But there is a problem with it, which we'll explore here.

Many causes have tried to do things like make their own 'ice bucket challenge'. This took social media by storm several years ago in 2014. Matt Damon, Bill Gates and even 'cool as a cucumber' Victoria Beckham took part. They filmed themselves being doused with a full bucket of ice water and challenged their friends to do the same.

What few people know is that this was originally developed for a relatively unknown cause. As the number of videos of folks taking a freezing shower grew to thousands, ALS (a charity that supports people with Amyotrophic Lateral Sclerosis, also known as Lou Gehrig's or Motor-neurone Disease.) worked with sports celebrities to 'own' the ice-bucket challenge.

They spread the idea that this gave participants a dose, however brief, of what it feels like to have ALS. Once people had taken the challenge, ALS asked them to donate, and challenge one or more of their friends to do the same.

The beauty of this idea was the striking visuals it created. But also, you have to admit, the schadenfreude of seeing a friend in discomfort and possibly being a little demeaned. Anybody could quickly prepare the challenge using materials readily available in their house, and it could be done in minutes.

All the ingredients were there for millions of people to do the challenge, and ALS raised over $115,000,000. Because it spread so quickly, charity workers assumed it had been easy for ALS to spark off.

Thousands of charities tried to recreate the same effect. They came up with their own challenges.

In the wake of this, one of my clients came to me with the idea of doing a 'barefoot challenge'. I warned them against the idea. Most of their donors did not value risk-taking and adventure. Not only that, their donors tended to be viewers of social media rather than active users. They were not used to taking videos of themselves on smartphones.

(The more alert among you will have spotted me using the MoVA formula here from chapter 4. You can use it to evaluate the potential effectiveness of any 'bright idea' that people bring to you for a fundraising appeal.)

Needless to say, the idea tanked. Not one person took up the challenge. Despite many weeks of effort, my clients made a loss. It was hard to bite my tongue and avoid saying 'I told you so'.

In fact, ALS had seen previous viral phenomena like the 'No Makeup Selfie' challenge that raised over £7m for Cancer Research UK.

They realised the way to capitalise on such things for fundraising was to have a rapid response team. They set up this team, who prepared plans and resources in advance.

They wanted to have people poised to be called into action whenever there was a viral phenomenon that appeared. If it was suitable to the cause, they could move fast to take full advantage. I suppose you could see them as the charity's own Batman and Robin.

This is the little secret not many people know about the ice bucket challenge. Viral phenomena actually require the kind of thinking, investment and preparation that most small to medium-sized charities don't have the resources for.

So, if that's the reality, why am I such a proponent of mass individual giving to increase your unrestricted funds?

Well, it's really quite simple.

Most people are doing it wrong.

Throwing out a cool challenge, a shiny shiny gadget – or any fun appeal that tickles your fancy – can lose you thousands of dollars and much wasted time.

The number one problem with trying to go big on one creative idea? It's useless without understanding your donors' MoVA: their motivations, values, and past actions.

Once you're pretty sure you've got a handle on those, test your assumptions and ideas cheaply and quickly. Even if you have to put them together with string and sticky tape.

As you've seen from the examples given, investing in your individual giving program can transform your non-profit. It can form a springboard to all these other types of fundraising:

- Major donors.
- Corporate partnerships.

- Legacy giving.
- In memoriam giving.
- Community or event fundraising.
- Donation drives.

I know how busy you are already. The reason you've gotten this far with the book is that you're curious to know how you can get out of the vicious cycle of too much work, for too little pay.

I want to show you how to target your investment of time and money, so you put in as little as possible, with as low a risk as possible, for maximum return. Then you can flip this to turn your vicious cycle into a virtuous circle.

Let's say you invest 4 days and £1,000 into your fundraising. This gets you back £1,200. So you reinvest that £1,200 into your fundraising activity again. But this time, you know the ropes. So you only need to invest two days. And because you've learned from your mistakes, this time around you raise £1,800. And you plough that back in. Now, it takes you one day and you raise £3,000.[4]

However, there's more.

Consider this: once you're OK at running appeals for people to give you one-off gifts (or cash gifts, to use our sector's jargon), try working on planned giving.

Let's say you invest 4 days and £1,000 into it. You make back £200 in your first month. (These are completely fictional amounts, just for the sake of argument.) That feels disheartening—you lost £800, didn't you? But remember, in just 4 more months you'll have made back your original £1,000. **And** the beauty of planned giving is the money just keeps coming in.

---

4   Of course there are limits—I don't think anybody could set up a great appeal in ten minutes. But if you keep going until you reach half a day per £10,000, that's where things start to get real.

If you are using the Values-driven Fundraising System, those donors will stay with you. So, within a year that £200 becomes £2,400. All the while you're reinvesting the monthly returns, with less and less time spent as you get better and more experienced.

As you keep this up, your unrestricted income grows and grows. You even get growth from the growth itself (like compound interest). Your steady growth begins to look like a hockey-stick graph.

As long as you're reinvesting some of the returns back into your fundraising, this growth can keep going until you've reached all the human beings on earth who share your values. My hope is you'll have fulfilled your mission long before that becomes necessary.

The exact system we use for this kind of growth here at the Donor Whisperer is the subject of the next section.

Key Learning Points from this Chapter

The problem with mass individual giving is that people think you just need one big cool idea and your crowdfunder or appeal will 'go viral' and hit its target. That's wrong.

You need to test out your assumptions about your donors' **MO**tivations, **V**alues and past **A**ctions. Even if you have to put your tests together with string and sticky tape.

Keep reinvesting the fruits of those experiments into your fundraising, learn, improve and try again. Pretty soon you'll have hockey-stick growth.

Part 2:
The Values-driven Fundraising System

Chapter 6:
The science of
values-driven fundraising

Take a look at this chap.

His name is Shalom H Schwartz, the man who developed the Theory of Basic Human Values. As it happens, I think he's a bit of a genius.

For years, he sent researchers into over 80 countries to interview people from diverse cultures, who spoke different languages. The researchers asked tens of thousands of folk about their values. If you think all human values are a 'societal construct' you are in for a shock.

The same values came up again and again.

I am hugely wary of "a study has shown" claims in books of this nature. However,In this case, Shwartz's research turns out to be very solidly replicable.[5]

Here's a picture of one outcome of his research:

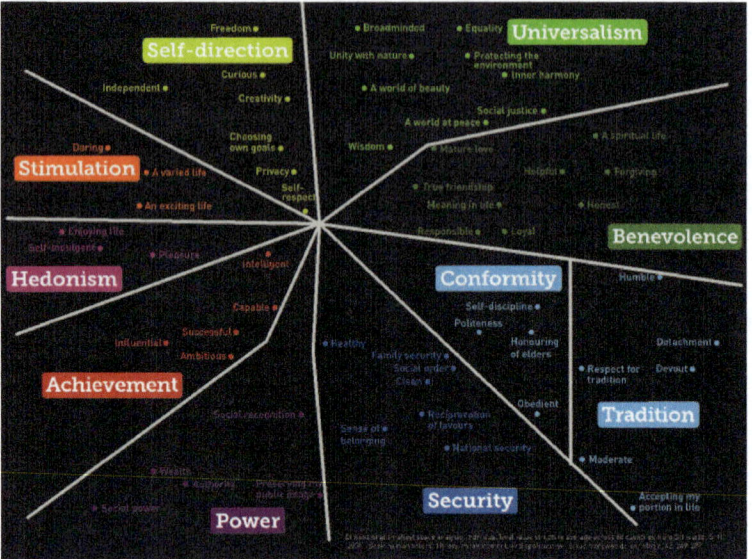

These appear to be values that people across the globe have said are important to them.

Values that cluster together are more likely to be held by the same person at the same time. Values that are far apart, less likely.

Values in the middle are more likely to be shared by everybody. Values on the outer edges of the map are less likely to be shared by everybody. (This shows us you can't pursue social power and social justice at the same time...)

---

5   As are all the studies I feature in this book. Ones that have been replicated across more than one country, at different times, by different researchers. Or I've replicated them myself. All where the findings are statistically significant— that is, mathematically unlikely to be mere chance.

Interestingly, when you get people to rate these values in order of importance, across cultures, benevolence always comes on top; power always appears at the bottom.

You'll see the map has been colour coded into blue, green and reddish colours. I give particular names to each colour grouping, to help my clients understand them.

While musing on this, I realised J R R Tolkien was prescient when developing his different mythical races for the Lord of the Rings books. Three of his races neatly describe the values in the green, blue and red spaces.

First, we have the Hobbits; the blue third of the map. (If you're not into Tolkien, but you like Star Trek, you might recognise Bajorans here.)

People who hold 'Hobbit values' might describe themselves as 'small c conservative'. They are driven by obedience and continuity. They respect tradition. They are the group of people most likely of all to say there are too many immigrants in their country. (This stays the same no matter how many immigrants there really are. Eeek.)

Now, if we move anti-clockwise around the circle, we reach the Elves; the three green slices of the pie. (For Trekkies, the way the human race is depicted like this.)

'Hobbits' can describe Elves pejoratively as 'Social Justice Warriors'. Elves feel strongly about values of universality, self-actualisation and social justice. All that tree hugging hippy stuff. (I say this as somebody who's partial to a bit of tofu myself.)

Finally, the red, purple and orange segments of the map share many characteristics with Tolkein's 'Dwarf' race. Don't let their stature fool you—these guys are going hard after fame, money and power. With a little bit of sex, drugs and rock 'n' roll on the side. (This roughly matches the 'Ferengis' in Star Trek and their obsession with gold-pressed Latinum.)

Dwarves like hedonism, esteem of others, trends, luxury goods, fancy holidays, keeping up with the Joneses. That sort of thing.

I suspect that you, dear reader, probably fall into the Elf category like me, because you're keen enough to have read this far.

You may notice that, like me, your natural inclination is to look down on the Hobbits and Dwarves, with their stubborn ways. But bear in mind that they may both look down on you, for being all 'holier-than-thou'.

There is a new way of thinking in the non-profit sector (in Europe at least) that worries me. It's been popularised by big organisations like WWF.

This school of thought says it's important to change the values of Dwarves and Hobbits to those of Elves. These values are seen as 'intrinsic' values and therefore superior to the 'extrinsic' values of the other groups.

Thing is—Elves would say that, wouldn't we/they?

This may get some people's backs up, but I believe it is unethical to try and change somebody's values. That way lies indoctrination and propaganda.

If a Dwarf came to me and said, 'I have started running a big campaign because I think your values are unethical and you need to start taking on my values', I would be outraged. But that's what some campaigners believe.

It's too easy to look down on people who hold other values to us. To think they need to change to be more like us. In truth, all these values work together to build a functioning society. If we had nobody interested in power, we'd never get anything done. If we had nobody interested in security, we'd be overrun by feral hogs.

The non-profit sector relies on values of benevolence, though. And that's a value the world really needs a lot more of right now, doesn't it? Yes—actually most of the world agrees with that, as we have seen above.

The problem is if your basic needs aren't being met, you'll probably hold values that put those vital physical needs first.

For example, people in countries that lack stability are more likely to hold values of respect for elders and security. This means they are more likely to get food and shelter, and survive. Children under the age of 11 will often report these same values. They are just learning to satisfy the physical requirements for life.

If we move clockwise around the circle to the Dwarves, these are mostly people who've been able to satisfy their basic needs. They have begun to look at improving their lot in life. They're interested in progress and money.

In countries that are rapidly developing like China, India and Brazil, we find this values group are in the majority.

Finally, those people who have not only got their basic needs met, but also have had the chance to start a career, buy flashy gadgets and go thrill-seeking, start to wonder if there's more to life. At this point, they are poised to take on values from the green area, and become Elves. They begin to think about how they can change the world for the better.

This may have changed since the 2020 pandemic, but the majority of people in countries like the US and the UK fit into the Elves category. (Last time I checked, it was a narrow margin, but Elves are still the biggest group.) If you're an Elf in one of these countries, this may surprise you. That's because you're still outnumbered by both Hobbits and Dwarves together.

Of course, all humans don't neatly into boxes like this and there are exceptions.

In the main, all other things being equal, these values are what drives human behaviour. And I'm sure you can think of people in your life who fit these descriptions quite well.

For example, I currently live with my 87-year-old father-in-law. He is almost an archetypal Hobbit. Each day, he does exactly the same things, from the food he eats to the TV programmes he watches and the shops he visits. He spends most of his disposable income on lottery tickets.

I'm a bit bewildered at this, because he has feet so sore they're a deep shade of purple. I want to call a foot doctor to come and help him, but he won't hear of it. He sees this as his lot in life; something he just accepts.

My husband, on the other hand, is a Dwarf. He is nothing if not ambitious; his top values are achievement and intelligence. (I like to think this is one of the primary reasons he fell in love with me…)

I love him dearly, but for some reason he really, really wants to own a Ferrari. I find this equally mystifying.

All my attempts at changing their values have been rightly snubbed. For one thing, it's patronising, and two, it's futile. People's values only change when their perceived needs are met.

Even then, it's not guaranteed.

This is a long and gradual process. If we attempt to change the values of thousands of people, it's like trying to boil the ocean.

So how does this apply to giving time or money?

People's values provide the motivations for giving.

Sometimes people will donate for reasons that aren't usual for their values profile. This happens if they are under certain pressures and in the right circumstances.

But in general, this is how it works out:

Hobbits / Bajorans

- Want to pay back a perceived kindness
- Have a personal relationship they want to maintain
- Have got into a habit of doing so
- To fulfil their traditions
- Want to protect others from suffering the way they or their loved ones have
- Need to feel they belong

Dwarves / Ferengi

- Are building or maintaining a particular public persona or identity
- Want to gain respect
- Are under peer pressure / expectation
- Want to get something in return
- Want to leave a mark on the world
- Will benefit personally from the cause succeeding

Elves / Humans

- Want a sense of agency in improving the world or their situation
- Desire to create meaning in their life
- Have a strong sense of compassion or injustice

This isn't an exhaustive list of giving motivations. You can probably think of a few more.

Now, why is this important? Well, when you get your potential donors' motivations wrong, you can waste tons of money and hundreds of hours on a misguided campaign or appeal. A misguided campaign speaks to a set of values or motivations that most of your supporters or potential-supporters simply do not possess.

Take one of my clients, a global human rights organisation. I encouraged them to create a hypothesis about who their future super-donors would be.

So, my client relied on a hunch. (This is a decent starting point when you create a hypothesis, but it isn't always right.)

They decided that parents working in the tech industry would be keen to become donors. My client thought these folks would give because of a concern about their children's future in a Big Brother world where privacy no longer exists.

I showed them how to test this hypothesis over a few days.

They discovered that parents working in the tech industry had other concerns and motivations for giving. I was surprised at this finding and so was my client. They went back to the drawing board.

In doing so, my clients avoided wasting tens of thousands of dollars and hundreds of hours of staff time on an appeal that would have been as popular as Liz Truss.

Putting the Values-driven Fundraising System into practice

In the following pages, I'll be walking you through all the techniques and strategies I use with my clients to explosively grow their list of potential donors. Then, in a short space of time, to multiply the amounts of money and time raised.

The order in which you implement these changes is important. If you start writing an appeal without understanding the values and motivations of your donors, it will bomb. Sometimes, even if you do understand these things, an appeal can still bomb, due to factors outside of your control.

So I'm going to show you how to minimise all the risks. You'll discover how to test things at a small scale, with tiny amounts of time and money. Then you can scale up only once you've proved something works.

At first glance, the moving pieces might be intimidating, especially if you are new to digital marketing, mass individual giving or campaigning. However, please don't let your knee-jerk reaction block you from seeing the long-term, recurring rewards this system can provide.

That said, you're a change-maker because you have, at the very least, a bit of fight in you. Embrace that now.

You can only hit new targets if you acquire new habits.

Key Learning Points from this Chapter

Different human beings have different values. In general, these values cluster into three groups which are more likely to be held by the same person at the same time.

- Hobbits/Bajorans: motivated by security, family, tradition and so on.
- Dwarves/Ferengi: motivated by esteem of others, status, power, adventure, trends, and so on
- Elves/Humans: motivated by benevolence, social justice, peace, new ideas, and so on.

If you fall into one of these values groups, you'll be motivated to give for different reasons than those in another values group. So, it's vital your non-profit understands, first and foremost, the values held by your best donors.

Chapter 7:
How to Make Values-Driven Fundraising Work for You

In this section, we'll dissect each step you need to take to make the Values-driven Fundraising System work for you.

I need to forewarn you: this process is simple, but it's not easy.

Whenever I sign a new client, I'm ecstatic. The reason is that they, like you, will get the key to avoid costly mistakes and keep growing forever. At least, as big as they want to.

Part of what makes this process hard is it's not always fun. (Oh, you'll have fun, alright! But some moments will—and I repeat, **will**—get you down.)

It'll be disheartening, for example, when you learn your pet theory about your future super-donors was wrong. Or your perfect idea for a new campaign would have made a tiny plop rather than a big splash.

I'll say to you the same thing I've said to many of my successful clients. Those same clients who are now giving their staff pay rises or hiring more people to join their team:

"Trust the process."

Sometimes, I even have to say this to myself.

Even though I've seen this system work time and time again, I'm still hard-wired to see failure as something to be avoided.

My teachers drummed this into me at school, and I'm guessing yours did too. But that culture—that fear of failure—has done us all a grave disservice. Failure is an obligatory step on the path to success. It is not something to be in terror of.

If the going gets tough, repeat these mantras:

'This is simple, but it's not easy.'

'Trust the process.'

Now you have the right armour to wear as you embark on this journey, let's begin with step 1.

1. The Donor Discovery System

Sometimes, when I watch game shows, I wonder why all the questions are so easy. (Not, it has to be said, when I watch the notorious BBC TV shows, University Challenge, or Only Connect. Those leave me feeling like a 7-year-old trying to understand quantum physics.)

As my Uncle said to me once when we were playing Trivial Pursuit: 'It's always easy when you know the answer'.

In the same way, this first stage of the Values-driven Fundraising System may seem obvious. Still, it's amazing how many non-profits skip even this basic step.

To find more generous givers, you must first understand what sort of people your existing donors are. Specifically, you need to understand their MoVA: their Motivations, Values and past

Actions in support of causes. Only then can you find more people just like them.

To start with, this means doing our own qualitative and quantitative research. Don't worry if that sounds complicated; it really isn't.

It's as simple as:

1. Interviewing six of your top donors
2. Running a supporter survey.

That's it; that's really all you need to do. At this point you may be thinking: "Ah, but 6 people isn't really a good guide to all those thousands more who are out there". That's a fair point.

Occasionally, my clients—especially younger organisations—find their interviewees are split across the three values groups. This is frustrating, but if it happens, trust the process. Record what you've learned—even if that's 'dunno'—and move on to the next stage.

As some of my smug friends like to say: 'Anecdotes are not science'. From our interviews and surveys, we will have a collection of anecdotes. What we need to do is make this all a bit more scientific, and thus, reliable. And we do that by using Facebook ads.

2. Secret Lightning Appeal Tests

I am not a fan of Facebook. I sometimes jokingly call it 'The Democratic People's Republic of Mark Zuckerberg'. It has all the power of a nation state and none of the accountability. I hope this will be resolved soon.

I still use it, with a heavy heart, and a big dose of defenestration (that itch you get to throw your keyboard out of the window). The reason I hold my nose and use it is that Facebook have made the most accurate and sophisticated learning system known to humanity.

Let's say I want to show a message to some people in Scotland who recently started a new relationship, are interested in photography *and* like 'The Shawshank Redemption'. I can do that very thing within hours. There's no other system in the world that allows me to do that with the same speed and accuracy.

What this means for you is, you create messages that embody the values you think your audience holds. You use Facebook to show these messages to your audience, and measure which message they respond to most readily.

The beauty of this is that the test only needs to run for 4 days for us to get a statistically significant answer. Imagine if you could have pollsters at your fingertips, and get an answer within days to any question you wanted, at a small fraction of the price? That's the power of Facebook.

Now, we don't always need to use Facebook beyond the confines of these tests. But because it's so widely used and so powerful, sadly—at least at this stage—we have to.

3. The irresistible lure

Next, we need to find a way to get these people's contact details.

To do this, you must get creative. Assemble your team and explain what you have found out about your top 20% of donors through your interviews, surveys and tests. Then, brainstorm together. (My editor tells me that brainstorming doesn't work, but later on I'll show you a method that avoids the pitfalls and problems with the usual methods.) Be as wacky, as daring, or as edgy as you like. Nobody's watching except your team!

Your aim is to find what I call an 'irresistible lure'—a sign-up mechanism that will entice your potential super-donors.

A great example of this is a recent brainstorm we held for my clients Students for Justice. I set out that this was a chance for them to get out their wildest, most creative, most yikes-y ideas. The idea was we wouldn't censor ourselves as we normally would in a work meeting.

We started a bit slowly with people being somewhat shy. I came out with a number of loopy ideas nobody would ever agree to, in an effort to get people to loosen up. Then up came some joke ideas. People started laughing. And we were away.

During this thirty-minute session with a handful of their staff, we generated over 100 ideas. Not only did we all have fun with the process, but everybody was delighted with the end result.

With so many great suggestions to choose from, we were victims of our own success. We had the tough task of narrowing these down to three most suitable 'lures'. The lovely side effect? My clients now have a smorgasbord of ideas to choose from for other campaigns.

As I write, we have just finished testing the top three for their current project. We used tools that were already available to them, or free, to create what I call 'string and sellotape' prototypes. They are not the finished versions of my client's 'irresistible lure'. But they were good enough for us to see which one is most enticing to their future super-donors. And it wasn't the one I expected, either...

Once you have found a winner, it's a case of refining the design, imagery, message and ease of use. The aim is to get the sign-up cost as low as possible; ideally below two pounds per person.

I say this because, in general, most non-profits are able to raise £1 per person on their list, per appeal. So, within two appeals you'll have made your money back. This is faster than most non-profits will recoup their costs when it comes to bringing in new donors.

If your cause is faith-based, or in service of animals, you're in luck. I've seen these causes raise £2 to £3 per person on their list per appeal. I'm always amazed at the generous nature of people of faith and animal lovers alike.

If you're seeking donations of time, this cost is less easily translatable, I'm afraid. You can always keep going with test after test, to try and get the cost per email address lower, or add in a few money asks to at least cover your costs.

Once you've done that, promote it to your existing email list and social media. Prompt your subscribers and followers to share it, too. This is one of the best ways to grow your list at no cost, because people are often friends with others who share their values.

Finally, it's time to find out which channel works best for your 'irresistible lure'. This will be the place where most of your super-donors have told you they hang out.

Look back at the results of your supporter survey in step 1. Rule out any that are too expensive or difficult. (TV broadcasts might be one of those, for example. You can always come back to that once you have enough money to invest in a test promotion.) Then choose the top two or three places or platforms. You may well be left with something like:

- Facebook
- Local newspapers
- Youtube

Or perhaps:

- Instagram
- WhatsApp
- TikTok

Run a test where you promote your 'Irresistible lure' on these channels at the same time. Make sure to use a different link for each channel so you can measure which channel brings you most new sign-ups.

Once you have your winner, this is the channel to keep investing more of your time and money in. There will come a point at which your sign-ups start to slow down, or the return on investment dips below 100%. At that point, reduce your daily budget, but keep it going.

You now have a wellspring of new donors! You can turn on the taps whenever you need more, and turn them off when you are overwhelmed.

You'll know the right audience, the right place to find them, and the right message to use. Congratulations! You've cracked the Giving Code. At this point, you'll be doing better than 95% of your peers.

4. Woo your future donors

Once your list is growing (or, even better, long before), you can start the process of 'dating' your future super-donors. Remember, before a person will give to you, they need to be able to affirm these four things:

1. I can see that this organisation share my values and give me a way to contribute that fits with my past actions.
2. I am motivated to give them my contact details.
3. I trust them to use my money, time or other resources wisely.
4. I can see how we have made a difference together.

If you've followed all the steps so far, then you'll have a handle on number two, and half of number one (this organisation shares my values).

Before these new folks will give, you need to focus on number 3; building up trust between you and your new contact (your 'date').

This involves doing the same kind of things you would do in what the sector calls 'a stewardship program'. You need to send them emails—single topic emails, once a week at least. For best effect, this could be a specific welcome sequence you send to them.

But not just any old emails.

These emails need to showcase your best achievements— campaign wins, stories of changed lives, animals rescued, volunteers overjoyed, milestones accomplished, legacies given, ecosystems protected, law-makers won over, celebs waxing lyrical about your work.

Remember which values category your best donors fall into, and make sure your emails speak to those values.

For example, Dwarves will be excited about you making the news, having exciting adventures, being talked about by famous or powerful people. Hobbits will want to know how you're carrying on or resurrecting old traditions, uniting families, keeping communities safe, conserving nature, and so on. Elves will want to know about systemic changes you've made, bridges you've built (literally or figuratively), new discoveries you've made, places where you've restored peace, villages you've brought sanitation to, unjust laws you've helped to repeal, and so on.

But remember—all the best relationships are two-way and between people. (My cats count as people, of course.)

Nobody wants to have a relationship with an organisation. (Unless that organisation has a particularly special brand with its own very strong character, like Disney or Apple).

Until your income grows to eight figures, it's unlikely you'll be able to achieve that level of universal recognition and fondness for your brand-as-person. So, what do you do before you get to that point (if you want to get to that point at all)? You make sure your donors get to know **you**.

Yes, you. The human being. With all your quirks, character flaws, foibles and turns of phrase. The real you, with your lovely accent. (Or, whoever in the organisation is willing to be the sender of the email.)

Ultimately, people give to people. Not organisations.

The more you can make this a true developing friendship (which, in a sense, it is), the better.

The other characteristic of a good friendship is that it's two-way.

Nobody wants to be *that friend.* You know, the friend whose name pops up on your phone screen and your heart sinks?

The friend where you plan an event 90 minutes after you meet up with them, so you don't have to spend too long making a concerned face as they moan about their life endlessly? Who's always asking for favours but seems to disappear when you're the one that needs a hand?

Don't be that friend. This new relationship you're setting up with your future super-donor needs to be **two-way**; as delightful as it is mutual.

That means you have great chats, an equal power balance and gifts that go both ways. When it comes to planning emails to your list, ensure to:

- Ask them about themselves (surveys, straight out direct questions in your email, polls, panel events where you take questions). Even up the balance by telling them your own story, thoughts and feelings.
- Take them on emotional journeys, using the full palette of human emotions (and yes, that does include humor, in the right time and place).
- Tell stories.
- Help them.

Wait, what? 'We're not building a list of beneficiaries here,' I hear you say.

I know. But you're still helping these potential donors in a lot of different ways. Remember, you are Yoda to their Luke Skywalker. Without you and your team, they won't be able to satisfy their desires for a better world, for themselves or others, depending on their values.

Helping them means giving them useful details or facts: guides, listicles, new findings. Explaining how you do what you do, and what's special about it. Telling them how much they mean to you, and how you're grateful for their time. (Yes, they might not have been intentional about giving time yet, but they are spending time reading your stuff. That's a lot more than nothing.)

5. Send compelling appeals

Once you've built up trust and you know they're still interested, you can take a big gulp and pop the question. Ask them to give their time or money, I mean.

But how do you know when they trust you enough?

I wish I had better news for you, but you can't know this for sure. The only way to find out is to ask. To make this easier, you can try a small ask first. If they say 'yes' to that, straight away, ask for the thing you really want. (This is known, rather unappealingly, as the 'foot in the door' technique.)

You may have seen a non-profit do this when they first ask you to sign a petition or pledge. Then on the 'thank you' page, they ask you for a gift of money. Or perhaps they request a chunk of your time—to write an email to your MP, for example. This is not the only way, but it's a good example and works well.

So let's get down to the brass tacks of what goes into an appeal people feel compelled to respond to.

If you're getting the hang of this, I hope you'll be thinking: 'Well, I have to fit in with my potential donor's values and past giving habits.'

But you need to make sure you get these elements right, too:

- Your giving mechanism must look, feel (and actually *be*) secure. That means, you put the donor's personal data under lock and key. Only they, and trusted employees, can know what it is. If this is online, show the logos or seals of the companies who provide your security certificate and payment methods.

- You need to spell out why you need the time or money. There should be a clear 'line of sight' from where you are now to where you want to get to with the donor's gift. In other words, if you're telling the donor you want to solve poverty in Bangladesh, and you need $2,000 for some boats, that doesn't make sense. It'll feel like a drop in the ocean. Your donor will be unmoved.
Instead, try telling the donor you want to help some families in one village pay for their kids to go to school. The way they'll do that is to go fishing in the boats you're raising money for. Now, that's better. It seems like a goal you can achieve together, and it makes sense. Your donor will be more motivated. They can see how their gift will make a difference.

A deadline helps here, too. In this example with the fishing boats, we could say that school starts in August, but the family have no money to pay the fees. There's a natural deadline.

Finally, one charity boffin (whose identity is lost in the mists of time) tested five words that will make a huge difference to your non-profit. I wish I knew who this person was, because they deserve a Nobel Prize for Fundraising.

What are those words? At the point of payment (if your donor is giving money) you give them the option for their gift to go to either:

- The fund that the appeal is raising money for [restricted funds] or
- 'Wherever the need is greatest' [any gifts allocated thus can be unrestricted funds].

This has worked on me several times. Not enough causes do it. Try it and let me know how you get on!

6. Build 'forever loyalty'

Your donor has now done the loving service of a gift of their time or money. It's time to cement their loyalty. For this, it's crucial you do two things, **and mean them.**

1. Thank them personally, from the heart.

To really wow your donor, you could record a video on your mobile phone. Imagine you're sending a message to a friend. Tell them how grateful you are, and what their money or time will make possible. It doesn't need to be long. Low production values are even better than high ones. The more off-the-cuff it feels, the better donors will like it.

2. Tell them how you've used their time or money, and show evidence of the results

By doing these two things well, you can do better than most of your peers. (Yes, really! In the rush and stress of getting out an appeal, it's amazing how many organisations then forget to tell their donors what happened next.)

Imagine if Game of Thrones had got cancelled half-way through, and nobody ever got to see the ending. (Here, please picture me making the face of the character in Edward Munch's 'Scream' painting.)

Don't do that to your donors!

As we've seen, even if things didn't work out, it's still worth telling the people who gave towards it. Remember the example of Charity:water? Donors can respond to failure with more generosity than they do with success.

Keep going through this cycle. Each time your donor gives, they see you using their money or time wisely, as best you know how. That's the way you'll win their heart forever.

7. Keep listening, learning and testing

It's not quite over yet.

There will come a time when you've reached all the super-donors you can. At least the group of super-donors you started looking at, with similar values and similar age profile.

Now, it's quite possible you'll have achieved your mission before that moment arrives. But it's also likely—if you have audacious goals—that you need to reach more people.

The way to do this is to repeat steps one to six with a different group of people.

Pivot slightly—whether that's to a different generation, or a group of people with different values.

The moments I've seen charities fail hardest at this is when they try to pivot straight to a much younger group of people with different values. Making such big changes is a mistake, as the more you pivot, the fewer existing campaign materials you have that you can reuse. The less you know about this new audience, and the fewer types of appeals you can continue to do successfully with them.

So pick one of these only:

- Same values, new age group;
  or
- Other values, same age group.

I'm going to sound a note of alarm here: the non-profit world has about twenty or perhaps thirty years left of 'business as usual'.

This is the time frame in which the Boomers—the richest generation who ever lived—will leave their legacies and go on to meet their Maker.

The good news is that the coming years will likely be a bonanza for you, *if* you're able to reach and delight these Boomers again and again, starting **now**. (And if you use all the steps I've outlined for you here, you will.)

The bad news is once they're gone, our current crop of big non-profits will see something like a 90% drop in income.

Why? Because many non-profits ignore how younger generations now give, and what makes them tick. (Some are wilful about this, some are complacent.)

The old models and structures of change-making worked in the 19th and 20th centuries. But they're now broken beyond repair.

However, all the steps in this book can help you to understand younger generations, and change the way you do charity.

So, keep having those intimate, two-way conversations with your donors, and others who come your way. Keep listening, theorising, testing and learning.

Repeat to fade…

Key Learning Points from this Chapter

1. This process is a bit of a roller-coaster. There will be ups and downs, but keep going and trust the process through these seven steps.
2. Talk to six of your top donors and send a survey out to the rest to uncover their **MO**tivations, **V**alues and past **A**ctions.
3. Scale up your tests to make them more scientific, using Facebook's advertising system.
4. Get creative and build an 'irresistible lure' that will compel your future donors to give you their contact details.
5. Woo your donors. Don't be '*that* friend' who is all 'take, take, take'.
6. On the small number of occasions when you do ask for something (relative to the times you give back), make your appeal compelling. Use a deadline that makes sense; make sure that the amount you want to raise feels achievable and will have concrete outcomes.
7. Repeat steps four and five to build 'forever loyalty'.
8. Keep having good conversations with your donors until you max out your learning, and the numbers of that group you can reach. Then, and only if needed, pivot a few degrees to a new but somewhat similar audience. Start again with step one.

Chapter 8:
Critical Components to the Successful Outcome

We started this part of the book looking at the science of the Values-driven Fundraising System. We went through all seven steps you need to take to go from 'first date' with your potential donor, to a fairy-tale wedding (sort of!)

Now, one key thing before you set off on this adventure to pay your staff what they are worth, and grow beyond your wildest dreams. I would be remiss if I didn't make sure you have the right kit for the journey.

These are the four things you'll need so you can get to your end point quickly and without injury:

1. At least seven hours of spare capacity a week between you and your other staff or volunteers.
2. Evidence of the good you do in the world.
3. Great stories and the skill to tell them.
4. Readiness to get your hands dirty.

When my clients have all these four pieces dialled in, they are surprised at what they can achieve.

Let's examine each to see if you have them—or if you don't, whether you can get there.

Staff capacity

To put all this into practice, you'll need about seven hours of spare capacity a week. If you can spare more—great! The more the better.

Some charities have whole departments of 50 people working on this stuff. If you need to grow that big to achieve your mission, you will get there. But only as long as you:

- Commit to following the process in this book.
- Reinvest a good chunk of unrestricted funds in growing your income.

If you don't have the capacity to spare just seven hours, you need to think hard about why that is. Search all corners of your mind. Be honest with yourself. Are you expecting too much, too soon?

Believe me, I know how desperate the need is out there. I feel it deep in my heart every day. So many hurting people, so many endangered species. It's easy to let it overwhelm you.

In fact, I have done just that. Not once but several times.

I have experienced burnout both physically and mentally. I have had Myalgic Encephalomyelitis (ME) twice and as if that wasn't enough, several nasty bouts of depression.

Now, there is evidence these are physical illnesses with biological causes. However, I do wonder if I was more susceptible because I put too much pressure on myself to be the saviour of the world.

As a (not very good) follower of Jesus, I'm kicking myself for doing over and over what my faith tradition tells me is the worst of ideas: thinking I can do Jesus' job. (Here's where, if I was talking to you in person, you'd see me shake my head and snort at my own sheer folly.)

If I had been more thoughtful about it, I would have realised the pressure to save the world—and to Do It Now!—came from my ego. It's pure egotism to think you're the only person, or organisation, who can solve the world's problems. 'If I don't do it, nobody will' = monstrous pride.

What a big-headed person I was. Sure, I have a role to play. There are others who are just as good as me who can take the baton next and run with it.

I want to inoculate myself against burnout – and I want you to do so, too. The vaccine I plan to take is to release the pressure on myself. I'll do this by listening to my body, by taking time out when I need to, by treating myself and by lowering my goals. (I say 'will' because I'm still learning to do this. In fact, I'm teaching myself as I type this.)

By putting this into practice, I know I will achieve more.[6] If I get this right, I won't have to rely so much on other people to look after me when I have nothing left in my physical and spiritual tank.

What I'm saying is—for the good of your staff, for the long-term health of your organisation, and most of all, your own sanity— lower your sights just a bit. Make your goals just that little bit smaller, and free up more space to invest in your long-term future.

You will thank me for it. And your staff will thank you for it, too, when they get a pay rise sooner than expected.

---

6   (Yet another one of life's weird paradoxes. Paradoxen?)

Evidence of the good you do in the world

All this is only going to work for you if you have evidence of the positive change you make. If you already have repeat givers, this is a good sign. It means they've seen enough evidence to be convinced you do what you say you will.

That could be in the form of your reputation, testimonials from your beneficiaries, before and after pictures, or something else. There is all sorts of evidence that can convince donors to give.

If you're struggling with this part of the picture (and even if you're not, because all non-profits could use more and better evidence) then get in touch with my team. We can tell you about a short and simple process you can go through to start collecting concrete evidence of the difference you make. This system is called the Transformational Index.

Here's what the United Nations Association (UK) had to say about it:

'Before working with the Donor Whisperer, the major challenge we faced was that we were not able to adequately measure our intended impact. This made it harder to persuade donors to invest in our plans.

Rachel worked with us on identifying our indicators of impact... It was great to be guided through the process and work together closely to figure out how to measure things that previously seemed intangible.

The ability to tell good stories

While some people are naturals, everybody can learn to tell spellbinding stories. I recommend, as soon as you've finished this book, you grab a copy of 'Made to Stick' by Chip and Dan Heath. It will show you how to craft messages that get lodged in people's minds and shared with others.[7]

Now, it could be you who tells the stories, or it could be a member of your staff who has a way with words. It doesn't matter, as long as your story-teller is consistent.

Stories are the lifeblood of your comms, especially when it comes to mass giving. And the wonderful thing about stories is the more you tell, the better you get. This effect is magnified if you practice, listen to feedback, learn, then adjust as you go.

Readiness to get your hands dirty

No, I don't mean gardening. (Unless your donors enjoy that, then maybe.)

What I mean is, for this to work, you must be willing to talk to your biggest fans. Those people who've given the most or for the longest time. You need to be open to hear things about why they give – or stop giving – that might be confusing or cause you discomfort. More on this in the next section.

You must also be ready to take a big gulp and ask people directly for money or time.

Hey, you're running a non-profit. It's what we do.

And, once you take on the fundraising mindset, you'll realise how much of a joy this is. Being the conduit for people to do good in the world is the most satisfying job in the world.

---

7   I also run a 'More Effective Copywriting' course. It gives you practical exercises on that and other elements of good storytelling, especially in our age of multiple distractions.

Key Learning Points from this Chapter

There are four vital elements you need if you want to grow your unrestricted income:

1. Staff capacity of at least seven hours a week. If you don't have even this, ask yourself why? Are you expecting too much of yourself and others in your team?
2. Evidence of the good you do in the world. This takes many forms, but donors need to be able to understand and trust it.
3. At least one person who can tell riveting stories about the difference you make.
4. A willingness to get your hands dirty—to talk to your best donors and hear what they have to say even if it causes discomfort.

Part 3:
How to crack your non-profit's Giving Code

Chapter 9:
Get to know your donors using the MoVA formula

We've already seen how crucial this is for increasing your unrestricted income. It's the first step in the Values-Driven Fundraising System. Here, I'm going to lay out in detail how to do it.

Now, I know this is hard. But I have lots of good news for you:

The first bit is you can get somebody else to do most of this for you. In fact, in some ways it's even better if an outsider does at least some of it. If people know they're talking to a senior person in the non-profit they're giving to, they'll probably tell you what you want to hear. They'll sugar-coat the truth a bit, at the very least.

If the person asking questions is more junior, or a freelancer, or works elsewhere, they will relax and say what they are really thinking.

That said, I strongly recommend you talk, face-to-face if possible, with at least two of your best donors (of time or money). Or at minimum, watch recordings of the interviews.

The second bit of good news is that even just the act of interviewing can sometimes prompt people to give to you.

For example, I once interviewed a donor on behalf of a client in the environmental sector. This was during the pandemic, so it took place over Zoom.

I could tell the person I was talking to was one of those people that I would call 'quietly wealthy'. The sort of person who knew if he displayed his wealth ostentatiously, this would mark him out as a target for con artists, thieves or fake friends. But if he just blended in with most other folk, nobody would suspect a thing. Like one multi-millionaire I worked for, who carried his laptop in a plastic bag. That sort of person.

As the interview progressed, he told me how he kept a spreadsheet of all the causes he gives to. He broke off for a few seconds to open it, to check how much he was giving to my client. (My inner geek was seriously impressed with this.)

And he became a little flustered because he realised his planned giving had lapsed. He said, 'Oh dear, I hadn't realised this. Hang on a sec…'

He went quiet and frowned a bit.

'I'm just going to their website to set it up again,' he said.

So, not only did my client get a donation; they got back a recurring gift from a wealthy person. That's the power interviews can have. And that's not even the best part.

Getting to know even as few as six of your best donors will lay a solid foundation. On this foundation you can build a secure future for your non-profit.

Why the top 20% of your list is important

When you start this process, it's best to look at the top 20% of your donors. (Or, if you're in the enviable position of having more than several hundred donors, then look at the top 10%, or even the top 4%.)

Why do I say this?

For the answer, we need to go back to Italy in the late 19th Century, and this dude:

Quite apart from anything else, that is a beard worth cultivating.

Meet Vilfredo Pareto. He was one of those irritating people who excel in many fields of study. In his case this included economics, sociology, philosophy and civil engineering. Among other things, you can blame him for inventing the concept of 'the elite'.

While at the University of Lausanne, he was studying wealth distribution. He discovered 20% of people in Italy owned 80% of the land. He was surprised at this and wondered if Italy was an anomaly. So he studied the wealth distribution in other countries and found it was similar to a striking degree.

When you plot these distributions on a graph, it makes a shape that resembles a really wide champagne saucer. Remember that image. (And try not to focus too much on the contents of the glass....)

This is sometimes known as the 80/20 rule, or the Pareto Principle. It's not always 80/20. Sometimes it's 95/5.

Let's say you make a spreadsheet of all your donors and list the amount they have given in their lifetime in one column. (It's easier with money, but you can also do it with time.)

Then, sort the spreadsheet so the person who has given most is at the top, and the person who's given the least is at the bottom.

If you add up all the contributions from the top 20%, I would expect to see these add up to around 80% of your income.

This works like a fractal, as well. So, the top 20% of that 20% (or 4%) may well give 80% of that top slice of income. Yes, I know that's a bit confusing but bear with me.

What I want you to do is to get to know the top-most of your top donors, if possible. Because we want to find a lot more people like them. And we are blessed, because modern tech means we can now do this faster than ever before.

How to carry out this research

There's a lot of good news here.

However there is one catch. What questions do you ask your best donors?

This is where people can easily go off-beam by trying to use their own 'common sense' (whatever that is). I've even seen big market research companies fall into this trap, which boggles my mind. Ask the wrong questions and you will get unreliable, misleading findings.

One of the traps is to ask about hypotheticals.

If there's one thing human beings are bad at, it's predicting their own behaviour. Just ask anybody who has made a New Year's Resolution.

Despite this, I still see researchers make the classic mis-step of asking, 'Would you do x?' or, 'If you saw this, would you…'.

This is why polling can go so wrong, because pollsters ask, 'If there was an election tomorrow, who would you vote for?'. A lot of people don't know which box they'd tick if they went into a polling booth now, never mind tomorrow.

The best guide to future behaviour is past behaviour.

Any questions you ask, whether via interview or mass survey, will give you way more reliable results if you ask about the past. (Don't get me wrong; I do believe people can change. But that's a tough process you can't rely on.)

Now, here's something a bit strange about asking questions regarding the future: these can make it more likely the respondent will do this thing later on. It's really a persuasion tactic rather than a decision-making tool.

So, if you have previous research where you made this mistake, take your hand off your forehead. These questions and the answers to them can still be helpful. If you asked about future behaviour, that will have increased your supporter loyalty.

In the end, though, for the purposes of this step at least, it's best to focus on what a person has done in the past. That's the most reliable guide to future action.

All the most useful questions (ones that elicit reliable answers, at least) must centre on finding out people's motivations, values and past actions in support of causes.

In an interview scenario, sometimes this can be difficult.

Some donors are strict about following the Bible verse 'don't let your left hand know what your right hand is doing'. Others want to avoid virtue signalling. This extends even to somebody from the very cause they have given to!

I like this a lot—it shows people often give for selfless reasons. Giving is a highly personal matter in many cultures, and that's good for all of us.

But what can you do to get your donor to loosen up and start talking about personal stuff? Look at the interview, especially one with a person you don't know that well, as an encounter where power is in play. You, the interviewer, have a lot of power because the act of asking questions puts you in the role of authority.

What I like to do, if I'm finding my interviewee is aware of this power imbalance, is to even things up a little. I'll give away some embarrassing or personal detail about myself. This establishes a norm, and if it all goes wrong, at least they have some blackmail material.

I might say, 'Last week I gave some money towards helping a hapless friend who fell 80 feet down a gorge. He needed some headphones to keep him entertained in hospital. I partly gave in awe of the fact he was still alive'. (Which is, in actual fact, true).

I'll also reassure the person that anything they tell me:

- Will be anonymised.
- Is in confidence.
- Shall only be used for the purposes of research to grow the fundraising for the cause they support.

There's a bit of a line to walk here, as you don't want to make it a leading question by accident. By telling my own story, I might get my interviewee thinking only about times they've given to friends, rather than causes.

So, I like to avoid doing this if I can. Sometimes, though, you may just have to. If you think there might be something missing, you can also prompt them to think about organisations they've given to in the past.

Now you might think if you want to find out a person's motivations, you need to ask 'What motivated you to give to x?'.

This won't help you, as most of us haven't a clue what motivates us. Or we **think** we know, but in fact we made a decision based on feelings and then only afterwards came up with a more logical reason for it. Or a reason that makes us look good.

The best thing to do is ask about what a person was thinking and feeling at the time they gave. This will give you a bit more insight than if you just ask directly about motivations.

The same goes for values. A lot of us pass through life without thinking about values.

I would be astonished if somebody said, 'Well, I value national security, which is why I give in support of injured veterans'.

What they might do instead is talk about how their grandad was in the Vietnam War and was devastated by how he was treated when he got home: not as a hero but as an outcast. This kind of answer shows the interviewee is firmly in the Hobbit category of values; their giving is driven by family dignity.

One of my clients was puzzled by this part of the process. They couldn't work out how asking questions about past giving behaviours would reveal a person's values. They didn't tell me this at the time. 'Trust the process', they told themselves.

I couldn't have put it better myself!

When we looked through the answers together afterwards, my client told me they were surprised how the values came shining through.

When I'm interviewing people, I also like to ask about negative experiences.

Questions like: 'Have you ever stopped volunteering for an organisation? What was it that prompted you to do so?' or 'Have you ever cancelled your planned giving?' can often reveal more than positive queries. One of the surest signals to a person's values is when an organisation violates them.

If somebody tells you 'I stopped giving because I couldn't afford it', ignore that answer. Unless they were literally about to be evicted from their house, this is unlikely to be the reason. It's code for 'I no longer felt strongly aligned with this cause' or 'It was no longer my priority'.

People like to bring money into the picture when they don't want to talk about the *real* reason. It's the same when people tell you 'I don't have time for X'. What they really mean is: that is not my priority right now'. It's easier to question the latter.

So, what do you do if somebody gives you this answer? Sometimes you just have to leave it, and infer their values from other things they've said. If you sense there is more they might be willing to tell you, you can always ask 'What were you thinking and feeling at the time?' or 'Were there other causes that you have given to since?'

This leaves us with past actions.

When it comes to a person's support of causes, their methods of giving are often habitual. Some people will only give their literal spare change, into a tin. Some will only give by credit card online. Many will send a cheque in the post. Others prefer to give time by volunteering at a soup kitchen, and still others will spend hours making memes to share on social media, or talking to their political representatives. So it's fine to ask 'What sort of things have you done in the past to support your favourite causes?'

I can't leave this subject without having a word with you about focus groups.

I have never understood market researchers' fondness for these contrived set-ups. I prefer not to interview people together, as is usually done in focus groups. I find 'groupthink' becomes a problem. People tend to modify their answers to look good in front of each other. This happens more often where there are power dynamics at play, such as with families or colleagues.

So that's the qualitative information (data about quality) you can get through interviewing.

Then there's the quantitative stuff (data that's easier to apply numbers to). You can get this by running a simple supporter survey. I like to use Typeform (at the time of writing) because it's such a joy to answer questions on their system. Some non-profits prefer to save money and use Google Forms. And there are many other systems available of varying cost and user-friendliness.

When it comes to demographics, I ask about age and location (rural or city-based). I need to have strong reasons for asking for any other details (such as gender or job title). This may seem strange to you, because so many marketers teach that you need to ask for gender at least.

I have lots of problems with asking about gender and job title. None of them are good guides to a person's values. They also lead us down the dark path of relying on, and thus reinforcing, stereotypes.

Age and location are the best guides to a person's values.

You could say 'birds of a feather flock together'. Folks tend to gather around others who have similar values, and this trend is most obvious when it comes to urban areas vs rural areas.

I ask about age because people who go through landmark events at a certain age will often be affected in the same way. (A stand-out example is 9/11, where you can remember exactly where you were when it happened. It changed everybody's world.)

A government's learning and fiscal policies have an outsize effect on a person's values at the age when they are introduced. So, age has a strong bearing on values.

Then, it's crucial to ask about media habits. I don't like to ask about these in interviews because, to be blunt, it's tedious. There's a long list of things you need to go through, one by one.

A survey is a better format for this because it's just a lot easier to read and tick boxes. I guide my clients to ask a question like 'Which of these do you use at least weekly?' (Tick as many as apply to you.) And then present options such as:

- TV
- Radio
- Podcasts
- Facebook
- Twitter
- SMS
- WhatsApp
- Messenger
- Telegram
- TikTok
- Clubhouse
- Reddit
- YouTube
- Local newspapers
- National newspapers
- Magazines
- Google
- Bing

And so on. It helps your respondent if you can group them together in terms of type of platform. So, for example, you could put Telegram, WhatsApp and Messenger in one section. Using icons also helps with speed and recognition and makes the experience more fun but can be time-consuming to set up.

Answers to this one will be vital later in the process when we look at testing which channels to use.

Beware of asking too many probing questions about personal issues without providing pointers, in plain English, to how you'll use the answers.

For example, let's say you want to ask: what is your income bracket? This is vital as a precursor to learning who it's worth sending a legacy campaign to, for example. But asking it without saying why can scare people. (And it's against the law in countries that are signed up to the EU's General Data Protection Regulation.)

Try to make your survey as short and fun as you can.

Yes, it is possible to make your survey fun. For example, with one client in the politics sector, we chose to ask 'Who was Prime Minister in the year you were born?'. This replaced the usual 'what is your date of birth?'. Thus it became relevant to the topic, and it stood out from other boring surveys.

It's also nice to present your supporter with other things that are fun to answer, such as:

- Which of these covers for our annual report do you like best?
- What is your favourite animal?
- What are your political pet peeves?

Finally, you **must** test the survey before sending it. You may well have supporters from marginalised groups. (Such as: LGBTQIA+ people, those for whom English may be a second language, and people with disabilities.) Unless you are in one of those groups yourself, you may not be aware of their needs.

How to run lightning appeal tests (audience, messaging, channels)

I've already touched briefly on how to run lightning appeal tests. But here, I'm going to walk you through exactly how you do it.

Facebook wants to persuade you to use their ad system, and they want you to spend as much money as possible. To do this, they ensure you get decent results. However, it's also in their interests to herd you towards using it the way *they* want you to. This may not be the same thing as what's best for your cause.[8]

There will be moments where the Facebook interface pleads with you to take a particular course of action. Ignore the robot's cries! (If you've ever seen The Good Place, think of it as 'rebooting Janet'. If you haven't seen the Good Place, then you need to fix that. - But only after you've finished this book, clearly.)

Now you have this book, you can avoid a common pitfall for those who want to use Facebook ads. They think, 'I just need to pick my audience, show them our message, and Facebook will work its magic, and hey presto! Donations.'

It *can* work like that. But it will be expensive.

---

8   I know it looks like I'm being unkind to Facebook. [Pauses to play a miniature violin here). In reality, anybody who needs to make a profit will be at the very least biased towards this rather than others' needs.

If you want to be wise in using your donors' money, take the following steps, in this order.

Audience confirmation test

What you need to do first, is test exactly which audience will work best for you. You do this by creating an ad campaign. You display exactly the same ad to each audience, and you see which audience engages most with your ad.

(Ideally, we'd want to test on donations at this stage. For some of these audiences, though, this may be the first time they've come across you. And like we've seen already, you don't propose on your first date. You only ask for a donation from a person once you've got to know them a bit.)

So, when you set up this campaign, choose 'engagement' (no, not *that* sort of engagement— oh dear, I chose a confusing metaphor for this bit, didn't I?) as the aim of your ad. And you want to go for Page Likes or Post Engagements.

There are quite a lot of ways to create audiences in Facebook:

1. You choose the detailed targeting options that fit the audience you think will be your best donors.
2. Use your existing Page audience.
3. Ask Facebook to find more people who share lots of data points (a Lookalike audience) with:
   a. your existing Page audience;
   b. people who've visited your website or even donated via your website. (You'll need to have a Facebook pixel installed and configured for this to work);
   c. your actual donors and supporters (by uploading people on your email list).

4. Select a really broad audience and let Facebook's algorithm figure out which people would be best to show your stuff to.

In an ideal world, you would test all of these against each other. But you might not have enough people who Like your Page. Or you might not have the Facebook Pixel installed, or you might not be able to upload your email list. That's ok. It just means it will take us a little while longer to home in on just the right audience for you. (And in the meantime, by following this process, you can start to create those audiences.)

It's annoying, but Facebook limits you to five audiences per test. So, if you're lucky enough to find that:

- your Facebook pixel is already set up,
- or you have a list of donors and supporters already in there

then don't bother testing on an audience of people who have interacted with your Page.

For some non-profits I work with, we just have to start with the broad audience and the detailed targeting audience. But the more different audiences you can test, the better.

If you are able to create audiences based on your email list, or even better, your donors, this can give you a benchmark to test any new audiences against. So do that if you possibly can (but first check that your privacy policy enables you to do so).

When it comes to detailed targeting options, Facebook can be a bit weirdly sneaky. Why they do this I'm not quite sure, but when you search for different interests or behaviours in their advertising interface, Facebook will hide a good deal of them from you.

So, for example, they might not show you 'Classic cars' unless you select 'Cars' as an interest first, and then click 'Show suggestions'.

However, I have a tip for you here. There's a website called audiencebuilder.io that will show you every single one of Facebook's 'interests' options. Have a look; it's totally free. I often use it myself.

While we're on it, I want to save you from a trap I fell into. When I first started targeting by interests on Facebook ads, I thought if Facebook said somebody had a particular interest, it meant the person liked that thing. Oh dear, how wrong I was.

Alas, I once innocently picked 'Islam' as an interest for an ad campaign. Facebook showed my ad to a lot of people who wanted to talk about Islam, but not because they like the faith. You can imagine the kind of comments these people made.

These days, I try to be clever with my 'exclusions' to make sure I only get people who are favourably disposed to the interest I mean. So, for example, if I want to advertise to vegetarians, I will choose that as an interest. But I also make sure to exclude people who like steak. Otherwise I am going to summon up more trolls than a big stone bridge over a dark swamp.

Now, create a Campaign in Facebook's ad manager. Create a different ad set for each audience you want to test. Then use the same ad for each ad set. This ad needs to be either:

- A recent Facebook post that got the most positive reactions, shares and comments from your followers;
- An image with text that sums up your core mission.

This doesn't need to be perfect. In fact, in some ways it's best if it's not your finest ever work. Why? Because we want to find the audience who are so attuned to what you have to say, that they'll respond to your message even if it's not beautifully crafted or the picture is a little out of focus.

You will only need to run this Campaign for 4 days, on average, to get a statistically significant result. A daily budget of £10 for each Ad Set should be enough. Many of my clients find they spend a lot less than that to get a winner.

Then, use Facebook's Experiments feature, and choose the ad sets you've created. When Facebook asks you if it should end the test early if a winning set is found, say no. As your test runs, **ignore** what Facebook tells you about your winning audience.

Facebook thinks you want the cheapest audience. You do not. You want the audience most predisposed to your message, which is not the same thing. An expensive audience might be better for you.

(This is clever on Facebook's part, because it's harder for them to sell ads to 'cheaper' audiences, and it makes it feel like they have your best interests at heart. In some cases they do. But Facebook's algorithm was trained on people buying products, not making donations. So you need to bear in mind that you already know more about how to do fundraising than Facebook's algorithm does.)

I've run these tests many times with all sorts of different clients. Sometimes Facebook's algorithm wins. Sometimes it doesn't. This is why running these tests, and in this particular order, is so important, because you can never predict which audience is going to work best for your cause.

Once your test is finished, you need to check whether the results are statistically significant. To help you with this, I have a specially commissioned, custom-built spreadsheet you can use that does some fancy calculations.

Download that here.[9]

Doing this is a key part of the scientific method. It helps us to know whether your results are just a fluke, a quirk of the data, or whether they are reliable. That is to say, if you ran the test again you'd get the same winner.

It's surprising how many actual 'scientific' studies aren't statistically significant. Yet they get talked about, or worse, reported in the press, as though they have sound findings. (At this point, you can picture me pounding the wall in frustration.) This is why people moan about 'science telling you one thing and then another'; not all studies are created equal.

But we do good science here, you and me, right?

Message test

Here is where you take the hypothesis about what your best donors' values are, and you test it at scale. As we noted before, six people isn't science. Yes, we have some good qualitative data from them. But it would be a tough task to interview enough people to come up with scientifically valid findings.

This is where the magic of Facebook ads comes in. We are going to use their system as a kind of infinite lab of human behaviour.

So, once you've got a winning audience from your audience confirmation test, we can be confident this is the group of people most attuned to your cause.

What you are going to do now is show this group of people different messages that embody the values you uncovered in your donor research interviews. Then, you can see which

---

9   https://whisper.ist/significance

messages get the most engagement, or most visits to your website.

Most of my clients find their interviewees share similar values. However, some are split between two different values groups. This test will help you to discover which values group is the largest among the people most predisposed to your cause.

For example, let's say you conduct six interviews. Of those, at least four people say they started giving because they were angry.

When you probe further, they say things like 'It's unjust what these people have suffered' or 'I feel guilty that I have such a charmed life and these folks don't, through no fault of their own'. And the other two interviewees say they started giving because their friends asked them to.

I hope you're there ahead of me, but it looks like—so far at least—your best donors are Elvish, but you have some Dwarves too.

So, you want to craft two messages—one that puts across Dwarfish values, and one that is most like what an Elf would say. You can even pull out a quote from one of your interviews if you like.

Here is what this looks like in practice, for one of my clients:

His parents told him not to come back home.
This is how leprosy destroys lives.

"This is a place where miracles happen," said
Pam Rhodes after visiting this leprosy hospital
in Nepal.

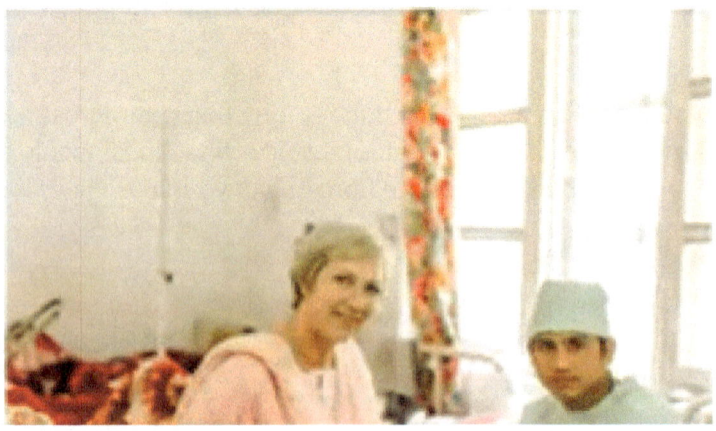

The first advert is aimed at people with Elf values. It invites us to
have compassion for the injustice and heartbreak suffered by
this young man.

The second is aimed at people with Dwarf values. (Pam Rhodes is a TV presenter who is famous in the UK, where this client's donors are mostly based.)

What's great about this kind of test is that you can use it not just for testing values and motivations, you can use it to test other things as well. Anything you're curious about, in fact.

- Do pictures of families or children work best for your audience?
- Which animal is your audience more attracted to?
- Which kind of emotions work better to draw people in— hope, or anger?
- Does a button that says 'get access' or 'learn more' get more clicks?

Most of these you can come back to, once you've discovered which messages really press your audience's emotional buttons.

Once you have found a sure winner from the message test, you can be sure that message will work with the same audience no matter where they see it. Or even hear it. That could be in print, on a podcast, in a YouTube video, or on a billboard, and many more channels.

If you've used my statistical significance calculator[10] and it shows you don't have a sure winner, you have two choices:

1. Carry on the test for a bit longer and see if the numbers change enough for you to be at least 90% sure you can drop the losing values message(s).
2. Accept that these values are equally good for your audience.

---

10   Here's the link again just in case you missed it the first time: https://whisper.ist/significance

How to build your list using an irresistible lure

If it's not a good idea to ask a new audience to donate right away, what do you do instead? You pique their interest with something I call an 'irresistible lure'. This is something that's useful, fun, intriguing or emotional in some other way. It must cause your future donor to give you their contact details.

The most successful 'lures' provide something that satisfies your target audience's motivations and values.

There are so many different examples out there. Here are just a few my clients have used:

- A 'guess which Christmas card will be our best seller' competition with a 10% discount on the cards.
- A 'which super-villain are you?' personality quiz.
- A one-question poll.
- A free housing factsheet for people in the care system.
- A petition to drop the COVID debt that developing countries owe.

For example, one big charity I know of have seen explosive growth using Irresistible Lures that fit their audience's values. They came up with ideas for quizzes and turned their top ideas into minimum viable products. They built these simply using Typeform and tested them to see which topic did best.

Once they had found a winner, they used the platform Impact Stack for the winning topic – hidden plastics. At the end of the quiz they asked the user to sign a related petition on Impact Stack. They promoted the quiz using Facebook adverts and recruited over 50,000 new supporters! The average cost for each lead was 80p - £1.10. This is around half of the benchmark of £2 that I aim for.

With irresistible lures like quizzes as part of its digital strategy, the charity's supporter base grew rapidly from less than 120,000 contacts in Impact Stack to over 1.5 million contacts within six years.

Some charities rely on creative agencies to imagine and build such things for them. I used to run one of those agencies. We'd use a whole collection of tricks and hacks I learned from other creative people over the years. These would really get our creative juices flowing, and clients loved the ideas we came out with.

These days I want to teach you the creative brainstorming and testing techniques we used for clients like this. Then you can grow your capacity and not need to rely on consultants so much. So, I'm opening up the black box for you and letting you see everything inside.

I'm fully aware the word 'brainstorm' gives some people chills. One of your colleagues calls you into a meeting room to do some 'blue sky thinking'. They might write your goal on a white board, then simply ask people to come up with ideas.

The problem is people's brains don't work like that. If you've ever played a word association game, you'll know that the results are predictable. For example, if I say the word 'soap' to you, you might come up with 'dish', 'bubbles' or 'clean'. If you're in a cheeky or lateral thinking mode, you might even say 'Eastenders'. But it's unlikely you'd say 'carrot'.

Your brain works by making connections with adjacent subjects. Let's say your colleague demands ideas for a new campaign name. It's a tough call to come straight out with something that shines. That's going against the flow of your own thought patterns.

Another issue with the way brainstorms are often run is that they work against introverts.

As a raving extrovert, I don't know what I think until I start talking. For some, that looks like me firing off annoying amounts of nonsense, none of which is even close to a decent idea.

An introvert will close their mouth and focus on turning an idea over in their mind like it's a delicate ornament. They make sure it's at least a fully-formed sentence before the words leave their lips.

These two factors working together can stymie just about any 'ideas generation' meeting unless it's held in the local bar. (Once alcohol starts flowing, it dissolves our brain-to-mouth filter, and messes with the brain's usual connection making.)

If you're content to buy all your staff several rounds of drinks, then go ahead. (As long as that's culturally appropriate. If you have strict Methodists or Muslims on staff, please don't.) But first, there's a much cheaper and less coercive way to do this.

All we need to do is make a few tweaks to the way we run an ideas meeting.

This is best done with at least four people. Seven or eight is ideal. Once you've got them together, give them a bit of background. Tell them what you've done so far, and what you've discovered. I find that pulling out quotes from interviews, then showing the ads and test results will get people interested and excited about contributing.

Then, explain to them what an 'irresistible lure' is and what you want to achieve with it. You want their ideas: anything that pops into their head. Nothing is too silly, outlandish, wacky, or offensive.

For example, I used to teach this brainstorming process when I delivered training on writing emails that get a response. We would collaborate on coming up with ideas for a subject line that is short, emotional and salient.

On one memorable occasion, in the first few months after Donald Trump was elected, these are the suggestions my clients came up with:

Now, I doubt whether 'Well thanks, Satan' would have gone down well with this particular non-profit's supporters. But it did spark off other ideas that were, let's just say, 'more usable'[11].

You can go through the process of winnowing down the ideas later.

All that said, I haven't explained the important tweaks yet:

---

11   For other clients I think that might possibly work, who knows? Anyway feel free to steal any of these subject line ideas. Just promise me you'll split test them and let me know which one wins.)

Important tweak #1: Make a rule that this process is done silently. (Be aware that if this process is going well, people may start laughing. That's great!)

Use sticky notes (if in person) or a Google Sheet (if online) to collect people's ideas. When a person has written one idea down on a sticky, they pass it to the next person. Hopefully, the new note will inspire another idea. In Google Sheets, everybody can see everybody else's ideas instantly, so this should happen as a matter of course.

Important tweak #2: Split your brainstorm up into three rounds.

Round 1

The first round will be something I call 'Concept Jam'.

Open your browser and search for a random word generator, a random picture generator, and the Wikipedia random page generator. Press the 'go' button on each one.

Once you've done that, you'll have three unexpected concepts. Now show these to your brainstorm team. Explain they need to try and connect these together with your cause or campaign somehow.

For example, let's say your cause is about preserving ancient musical traditions. Your random concepts are:

Funny   Chains   Formula One Motor Racing

The concepts you might generate for an irresistible lure could be:

- Free comic about ancient instruments.
- Let's start a song-writing chain.
- If we had a musical race, which of these songs would win?

This is the round people find hardest. This is deliberate because it loosens up people's thought patterns. The ideas generated in this round are usually the least practical or useful. However, they create a fresh (if goofy) platform for the next two rounds, to broaden the creative horizon.

After 10 minutes, or whenever the ideas slow to a trickle, move on to the next round.

Round 2

In this round, you're going to do something I call Newsjacking. It stands for 'hi-jacking the news'. You're going to jump on whatever band-wagon is rolling by.

Beforehand, grab links to these three pages:

- The most popular news site in your audience's country
- A site where your top donors told you they get their news (taken from your survey)
- Twitter's trending page

The idea here is you can make a lure that's irresistible by using what your audience is already talking about. Although this lure may have a shorter life, it may work well to connect your cause to something that's already in the news.

Guide your team to pick one of these links and look at the headlines. See if they can come up with ideas or concepts that relate to the headline in question. This was how one client came up with the concept of the 'Good News Challenge'. Looking at the headlines about COVID-19 deaths made it clear to them that people were in dire need of cheering up.

Then, after ten minutes of this, or however long it takes before people lose momentum, move onto Round 3.

Round 3

Present the participants with this list of existing types of 'irresistible lure'. All of these have worked for other non-profits to build their lists.

A: Competition	B: Online event	C: Challenge	D: Discount offer
Example: Photo caption competition	Example: Q & A with a celebrity or expert	Example: A 'live below the poverty line for seven days' challenge	Example: printable coupon for 25% off in our shop
E: Personality test/what type of … are you?	F: Digital freebie	G: Game	H: Chatbot
Example: 'Which Star Wars character are you?'	Example: A free guide to protecting yourself against diabetes	Example: 'Thwack the mosquitoes to battle malaria. Can you beat your friends' scores?'	Example: 'Our bot will help you claim money back on your delayed flight'
I: Collective task completion	J: Physical freebie	K: Creative tool	L: Giveaway / prize draw
Example: 'Sign your name on this to add your piece to this jigsaw. What will the picture be?'	Example: 'Receive your free laptop sticker'	Example: 'Make your profile pic look like the famous Obama poster'	Example: 'Sign up to win Jurgen Klopp's baseball hat.'

M: Message of encouragement	N: Offline event	O: One question poll	P: Petition / pledge / handraiser
Example: 'Send a message of encouragement to a blood cancer patient.'	Example: 'Attend our refugee film festival.'	Example: 'Should we abolish the monarchy?'	Example: 'Sign the pledge to be a trans ally.'
Q: Test your knowledge quiz	R: Send an e-card	S: Something else?	T: Mini-course / email series
Example: 'Are you a true gourmet? Can you name all these exotic foods?'	Example: 'Decorate your own Valentine's day card to send to a friend.'	Example: 'Pledge to donate for your birthday'	Example: 'Take our free 5-week course on switching to a plant-based diet.'

Explain that in this round your team are free to add in other ideas they've had that didn't fit in the first two rounds. However, they must continue to write whatever comes to mind; there is no wrong answer.

Your colleagues will most likely be limbered up and enjoying themselves by this point. As this round is easiest, even for people who don't consider themselves creative, it's a nice note to end on.

By this time, you may well have dozens of ideas. You now have the rather wonderful challenge of narrowing them down!

You can do this all together right away. Or you can convene a smaller group to work on the process.

If everybody is hyped-up and you have the energy to keep going, I suggest you do something called a 'dot vote'. Each person in your team gets three dots (you can buy some little coloured stickers if you want, or you can hand out different coloured pens). Each person adds one dot to the ideas that fit these criteria:

- Quickest for us to make.
- Fits with our audience's values and motivations.
- Cheapest.

Once everybody has added their dots, choose one, two or three ideas with the most votes.

At this point, depending on how much time and budget you have, you could make prototypes of your top three 'lures'. Then test them against each other in the same way as you did for your lightning appeal test.

You can also do this by sending a split test to your email list. Each email would point to a different 'lure'. Then see which one gets the most extra sign-ups, both from your list and via sharing.

Or, if you don't want to spend the extra time, you could go straight for the overall winner with most dot votes (if there is an outright winner)

Here are some free or low-cost tools you can use to prototype your 'lure'. Then you can see how well it works before you put it on your fishing hook and cast it into the great digital pond. The letters correspond to the types of 'lure' in the table above that these tools are best for making.

A, M, O:
Typeform, SurveyMonkey, Google Forms.

B:
Zoom, Microsoft Teams, Google Meet, Facebook live, YouTube live.

C, D, F, J, L, O, T:
Mailerlite, Action Network, Engaging Networks, Campaign Monitor, MailChimp, DotDigital, Charity Email, Hubspot, Nationbuilder.

E, Q:
Riddle.

G:
Sploder, Flowlab.

H:
ManyChat.

I, P:
Engaging Networks, Action Network, Impact Stack, DoGooder, Nationbuilder.

K:
Twibbon, Pixteller, Envato PlaceIt.

N:
Eventbrite, Fienta, Engaging Networks, Nationbuilder.

R:
Engaging Networks, Impact Stack.

My friends at the digital mobilisation agency more onion have produced a free report with all sorts of tips for optimising sign-up forms. A sign-up form (where your potential donor provides their email address or phone number and opts in to hear more from you) is the lynch-pin for any 'irresistible lure', so this report is gold dust. Get the report here: https://whisper.ist/optimise

Once you've found a winner, or you have good feedback from it, test and refine the 'lure'. Your aim is to get list sign-ups at £2 or less.

Super tip: send the 'lure' out to your email list. Encourage your supporters to take part and then share it. This can get you hundreds or even thousands of new potential donors for free. It will also strengthen the bond between you and the people on your list.

Congratulations! You now have the 'new donors tap' that I have been talking about.

You should be able to raise £1 per person on your email list, per appeal. So, each of these new potential donors could pay for themselves within two appeals' time. That's the magic money gumball machine that we dreamed of earlier on in this book.

Now, just like that story, you may be tempted to throw all your money at promoting your 'lure'.

However, there are limits, sadly. What we've found is that if you spend more than £100-£150 per day on a Facebook campaign, the quality of sign-ups drops off a cliff-edge.[12]

So how do you expand the limits once you've maxed out the people you can reach on Facebook? You test different channels. Yes; in the same way you did with your audiences, your messages and then the different lures.

Pick the top two or three most popular channels from your donor survey. Promote your lure on each one and see which one gets you the most sign-ups.

In an ideal world, you would test the channels for exactly the same length of time, between the same dates, using the same words and the same format. Sometimes this isn't possible—just make the ads as similar as you can.

12   I expect some of you may be thinking 'well, chance would be a fine thing!' as you read this—but if you stick at this process, you will get to that place.

At the end of all this, you'll have cracked the Giving Code. You'll know:

- The type of people your best donors are.
- What message works best to grab their attention.
- How to get their contact details.
- Where to find more of them.

Key Learning Points from this Chapter

Getting to know your best donors using the MoVA formula is vital for any cause. By best, I mean the top 20%, or even top 5% of your best donors.

You'll need to do this using both qualitative (interviews) and quantitative (survey) research methods. Stick to asking questions about past behaviour and demographics (age and location are best; others matter less).

Then, scale-up your testing to make it more scientific. Run your tests in this exact order:

- Audience (which type of Facebook audience works best for you?)
- Messaging (to confirm which values this audience shares, and the message that works best to attract them)
- Channels (Is there a channel that works better for you than Facebook?)

Make sure to use the statistical significance calculator to double-check if you have really found a winner.

Chapter 10:
How to write appeals that push your audience's buttons

Now you've figured all of this out, and you've wooed your donors, you need to ask them for money or time in the most suitable way.

How people with different values give differently

As you might expect, our values groups are poles apart in what motivates them to give. I'm speaking in general terms here; some people will buck these trends. But for the most part, they are reliable.

Hobbits/Bajorans

People in this values-group may have a faith or religious tradition they want to uphold. For some, this is called tithing (as much as 10% of their income). For others, it may be 4%, or fixed gifts at certain times of the year.

It can be much easier to persuade Hobbits to give regularly as this is already part of a habit they have.

If there are popular cultural moments where people are expected to give, you'll find Hobbits are among the most generous givers.

My father-in-law, for example, gives beyond his means during early November. I probably don't need to tell you which cause, but it involves a red flower. He has done this for years.

Often Hobbits will give by cash or cheque. They like to keep their giving secret because they value modesty. Showing off their giving would be a total nightmare for them.

Folks with these values don't want to feel they owe anybody anything. So, if your cause has done them a kindness—for example, they got a benefit from your organisation in the past—it's worth asking them to support you with time or money. They'll be glad of the chance to 'pay you back'. For goodness' sake, though, avoid being explicit about it. A Hobbit would find that vulgar and off-putting.

So, if your best donors are mostly Hobbits:

- Provide ways to give anonymously.
- Allow them to give by cash, cheque or bank draft—whatever giving methods they're used to (for some this might be Paypal or credit card).
- Plan your appeals around traditional festivals or moments in their culture where giving is expected;
- Ask your beneficiaries to give.
- Prompt existing donors to ask their family and close friends to give or provide expected ways of doing so; 'in memoriam' giving, or jumble sales, for example.

There are some causes Hobbits don't often give to, such as human rights, foreign aid and causes that address structural issues. Hobbits like to give to charities based in their local area. Their support often goes to beings whom Hobbits consider less well off or less safe than themselves. Hospices, animal rescues, abused children, people with disabilities—these are all causes Hobbits are more likely to support.

Dwarves/Ferengi

As an Elf, I can't fathom why Dwarves would give, but they do. Dwarves, like Hobbits, can indulge in outrageous acts of generosity.

Dwarf motivations are so very different from Elves and Hobbits. If Dwarves have a chance to take part in a challenge, they relish it. It's a chance for them to garner the esteem of others that they yearn for.

Likewise, if a Dwarf friend is invited to sponsor another person who's doing a challenge, they'll do it. Not always because of the cause, but because it's a chance to show how loaded they are.

Dwarves are drawn to causes that are in vogue, especially if their favourite celebrity or coolest friends are involved. They want to bask in the reflected glory.

Before we met, my husband (the Dwarf I know best) once raised money for charity by shaving off his hair. He posted this on his online dating profile. (Naturally, being an Elf, this was one of the things that attracted me to him.)

Another fundraising tactic that works with Dwarves is if they get something in return. For example, you might turn their heads with a limited edition or collectible item that comes in exchange for setting up a direct debit.

Back in the early 2000s in the UK, there was a campaign called 'Make Poverty History'. If you supported the campaign, you could donate and get a white wristband. Chris Martin, the lead singer of Coldplay, was seen wearing one at a gig. Soon this became a big trend.

I remember wearing mine proudly because I loved the cause. A worker at the university where I was a lecturer asked me where she could get one. Her son thought it was cool—all his friends were wearing them, and he wanted one, she said. She couldn't find one anywhere in the shops.

I can remember being puzzled that anyone would wear one because of a fashion trend, rather than the cause itself. But since I learned about the different values groups, I now understand.

Another tactic that works with Dwarves is to offer them a high profile place their name can be placed when they give. This is one of the factors in Patreon's success—my guess is they are overrun by Dwarves. Often the person raising funds through Patreon will display their patrons' names on their website, videos, or creative works. This allows a Dwarf to fulfil their longing to leave their mark on the world.

Finally, Dwarves give to appeals where they will benefit if the cause succeeds. For example, if you're a green cause, there will be Dwarves working in the renewable energy industry who would support you.

So, if your best donors are mostly Dwarves:

- Offer something in return for a gift—naming rights, for example, or listing their name on your website.
- Host auctions for desirable items or experiences.
- Look into retail opportunities—greetings cards, pin badges, virtual gifts, t-shirts and so on.
- Create challenge events like marathons that Dwarves can take part in, or even better—compete in a team to see who can raise most money.
- Consider celebrity patrons.
- If it's within your means, host swanky fundraising events and invite all the 'cool kids'.

Dwarves are less bothered about the type of cause they support. Their big concern is whether it is a good one to be linked to, in the eyes of people they respect.

Elves/Humans

If you're reading this book, odds are you fall into this category.

A lot of Elves make the mistake of thinking we are the most generous givers or reliable donors of them all. Actually, we aren't.

We can be flighty—longing to make the world a better place but not always able to commit to one way of doing that. We may try all sorts of different things and give to multiple causes at once.

Elves do have an exquisite sense of compassion or injustice. We can be swayed by emotional stories, particularly if they're from causes that Hobbits and Dwarves don't care about so much.

Our heart's desire is to have a sense of agency in improving the world or our own situation. So, any cause will have to set out in exact terms how our gift will help, and follow through.

If your best donors are Elves, then:

- Make it easy to give.
- Explain your unique way of addressing issues.
- Follow up after an appeal or campaign to show exactly how you made a difference.
- Create personal connections between your donors and beneficiaries if possible.
- Ask for input and feedback.
- Offer different ways of contributing, whether that's advocacy campaigns, volunteering or giving money.

I'll admit I'm the sort of person who stops liking bands when they become famous. Elves like to think we're always one step ahead (and to be fair, we often are). We will champion causes other values groups can't understand or find confusing. We want to target the root cause of problems or address structural issues. If we're given the choice, we'd rather give to causes that prevent hunger rather than ones that only spring to the rescue when famine strikes.

Bear these in mind when you put together an appeal for either time or money.

Need some quick ideas for your fundraising campaign? My friends at Impact Stack have an ideas generator tool here:

https://whisper.ist/resources

Next, let's look at aspects of giving that work with **all** values groups. As humans, some parts of our brains do work in the same predictable way. I'll walk you through these, and how to apply these factors to your online appeal pages.

Key Learning Points from this Chapter

Once you've found the values of your best donors, you need to know what will prompt that values group to give. Some appeals will work better than others depending on whether you're talking to Hobbits, Dwarves or Elves.

- Hobbits like to give anonymously, and according to their well-worn habits. They are more likely to give according to tradition. They want to pay back a perceived kindness, or because close family and friends have asked them to.
- Dwarves give to get something back, or to prove how cool, strong, or daring they are.
- Elves want a sense of agency in making the world a better place. They'll respond well to being asked for input. They want to see how their gift made a difference. Elves relish the chance to do something unique that gets to the root cause of problems.

Chapter 11:
Anatomy of a great appeal/campaign page

Any great appeal or campaign will first and foremost be easy to use. Right the way through, from the social media posts to the thank you email.

To show how much this matters, let me tell you about the example of an international humanitarian cause. They used Impact Stack to run a test of their sign-up form. They wanted to see whether:

- having a tick box (which people could either check to opt-in or ignore), or
- yes/no radio buttons (where people have to choose yes or no)

would impact the sign-up rate.

Using a tick box resulted in a 15.3% opt-in, while using radio buttons increased opt-ins to 48.6%.[13] This was so successful that it led to others across our sector adopting radio buttons. You can read more about this in a free report here:

https://whisper.ist/tickbox

---

13   (Be careful with this, though! You might think that radio buttons should be used on all pages to boost sign-ups.

But after more tests, this charity found out that radio buttons decreased donations a little (by 5%). So now they use radio buttons where the goal is opt-ins. But they use a tick box where the goal is conversion - like donation asks.

Let's say you're a small org with few resources and you want to replicate this kind of success. My strongest advice to you is something that seems so straight-forward you'll wonder why you're not already doing it.

Find somebody who knows little to nothing about your cause, and would say they are 'not very good with computers'.

Visit them in a place where they feel most at home. This could be a favourite spot in the local caff, or their work desk, or maybe the living-room sofa. Ask them to respond to your appeal online. If an in-person visit is impractical, ask them to join you on Zoom and share their screen with you. Show them the social media post for your appeal or forward them the email about it.

Ask them to speak their thoughts out loud as they go through every step of the process.

My Mam is amazing at this because she says everything she's thinking in real time. She'll find strange ways of doing things and get side-tracked down rabbit holes while staying as polite as Postman Pat. (I know she'll read this so I'm just going to add here how I was right at the front of the queue in heaven when they were allocating the Mams.)

Use a screen recorder and mic for this if you can. I like to assure my volunteers testers that this is a test of the website, not of their abilities.[14] The more mistakes they make, the better, because then we can see what we need to fix.

The recording of this test will be worth its weight in gold pressed latinum. Why? To persuade your techies, or even the company that runs your donation page, to improve the process.

---

14   Whenever people hear the word 'test', they go into exam panic mode. Sometimes I have to say this more than once in creative ways—yes, it's great if you see an error message! Honestly!

One of my clients was working with a global payment processor who had been slow off the mark when it came to fixing bugs in their system. So, the project manager made sure to show this company the videos of people stumbling over the same problem. The testers said out loud what my clients were only thinking. After that, it got fixed in a jiffy that was jiffier than a jiffy bag.

I've been running those sorts of tests for over twenty years. Every time I run them, I'm always surprised how:

- Quite often there's simply one label or word that creates a stumbling block. And this ends up being easier than we thought to fix.
- People do weird stuff I never would have thought of doing myself. It's almost like they invent new forms of dumb-assery (technical term). Even if you've run several tests, it's always worth doing another one after you've changed something.
- Some organisations still haven't got their donation process to work well on mobile.
- It's rarely the graphic design of a page that stops people from giving. It's usually the coding or the copywriting that creates problems.

So, you've run some tests with real people. You've fixed the little issues that were causing people not to give or respond to your campaigns. What do you do now?

You can also follow this guide by my friends at more onion. They show how simple tweaks to your forms, from button size or text to form field design can improve your conversions. They also give you some ideas to test for even more impact. Get the free report here:

https://whisper.ist/optimise-donations

There are other things that will suppress your 'conversion rate'. (By this I mean the percentage of people who give once they've seen your appeal page.)

These are:

- No sense of urgency.
- Low response so far.
  Many donors, and Dwarves most of all, are not willing to give unless others have given first. You might hear people talk about 'social proof' and this is why).
- The ask is too general.
  There's nothing that shows me what's at stake. ('Donate today' gives me no information about **why** I should care.)
- Creating a sense of helplessness by making the problem feel un-fixable.
  Donors want to feel that change is possible. If they think their money will be just a drop in the ocean, you will lose them.
- The call to action is woolly, rather than specific.
- The page uses statistics rather than story as a tool to persuade.
- It looks inauthentic.
- The images are unclear or unemotional.

Let's have a look at those one by one.

Sense of urgency/scarcity

Now these are part and parcel of the same thing. Scarcity means physical resources that are limited. Urgency is a limited time.

Both things are known to motivate taking action in all sorts of contexts. It's why you see signs in shops that say 50% off for a limited time only. That increases the number of people who will buy.

You can generate scarcity by saying, for example: 'In this new coffee table book, we only have spaces for the names of twenty donors on the front page. Give more than £100 to make sure you save your spot.'

Here's another example. This is for a cancer charity in Australia.

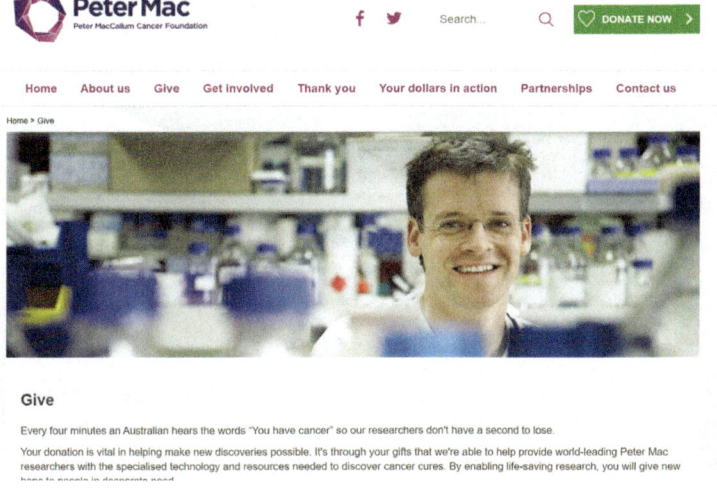

Ignore the smiling happy scientist. Yes, we want to feature scientists in the search for a cure for awful diseases. But this scientist looks fulfilled; like his work is complete. We don't want that when we're running an appeal of this type.

What I want you to look at here is the text at the bottom:

'Every four minutes an Australian hears the words 'You have cancer' so our researchers don't have a second to lose.'

You can almost hear the clock ticking as you read it. (It's also clever because it turns a dry statistic into a personal story; but that's another issue.)

Here's another example:

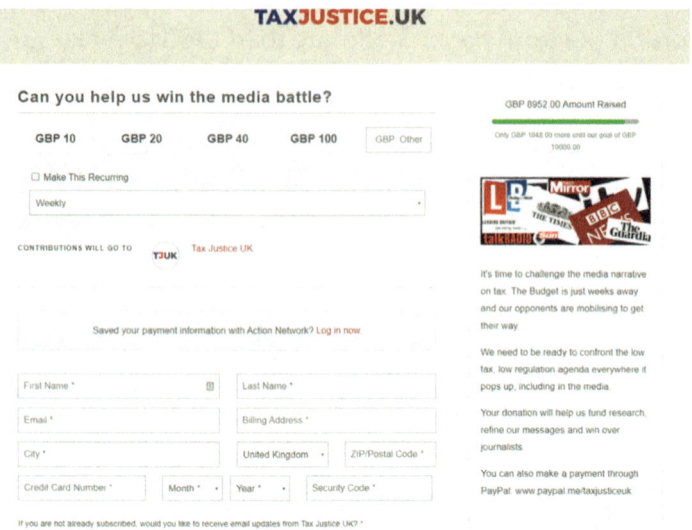

This is a client with a bit less money. They use a system called Action Network, and this is one of the standard forms it spits out. Their giving page isn't perfect by any means. But what I want you to pay heed to is the text on the right.

They're trying to challenge what the newspapers say about tax. The only time that this really gets talked about fully in the media is on Budget Day. So they're using that as a scarcity element to their fundraising.

Another thing that's powerful about this is that it looks at the threat; the opponent. There are other people like The Taxpayer's Alliance who want there to be as little tax as possible. So, you have the sense of an opposing force. We're in a race against them to reach the media.

Just for context; for some charities, £10,000 would be a small amount. For Tax Justice UK in their early stages of growth, this amount doubled their first year's income. I'm happy to say that, two years later, my client is now raising over ten times that in a year.

'Social proof'

So, next is a concept we've touched on before: social proof.

This is part of a big and growing field in science called behavioural economics. When I was at school, it was just called psychology. At some point the psychologists must have twigged that politicians were loath to sign off cheques for something that sounded so woolly.

Anyway, let's take off the spin; this is a field in psychology. And one of the masters of it is Robert Cialdini.

He is the author of *Influence—the Psychology of Persuasion*. It explains solid, replicated research on what motivates people to change their behaviour. It's well worth reading

One of the studies he conducted is called 'Crafting normative messages to protect the environment'. I had no idea what this meant until I saw the experiment.

It was all about trying to preserve a petrified forest[15] in the Escalante State Park, Utah. The park's problem was that visitors love petrified wood. People kept stealing it from the park at such a rate they lost fourteen tons every single year.

---

15   How does a forest become petrified? Maybe somebody told it about global warming.
Sorry, I can't help myself.
Actually, the process of petrification happens when plants are buried by sediment. Instead of decaying, groundwater that has lots of silica, calcite or pyrite in it (for example) flows through and replaces the plant material. This preserves details of the bark, wood and cells as a kind of fossil. It's pretty amazing stuff.

And so the park wardens, in their wisdom, decided to put up signs that read:

'Your heritage is being vandalised every day by theft losses of petrified wood of 14 tons a year, mostly a small piece at a time'.

One of Cialdini's researchers visited this park with his wife. She was a moral and upright person.

They stood in front of this sign and read it together. She nudged him with her elbow and said, 'Oh, we'd better get our piece quickly then', with a wink and a smile. He reports that he felt like saying: 'Who are you and what have you done with my wife?'

It was clear this park needed help. So they set up their own real-life secret lightning appeal test.

Cialdini's team put up these signs in the park saying:

'Many past visitors have removed the petrified wood from the park, changing the natural state of the petrified forest.'

They left this sign in the park for two weeks, and then they measured how many people had stolen the rare, precious wood from the park. The thefts doubled.

So, then, for a further two weeks, they put a new sign in the same locations in the park:

'Please don't remove the petrified wood from the park, in order to preserve the natural state of the petrified forest'.

This time, thefts fell by half!

We as a human species look to see what others are doing to understand how to behave. The first sign tells us that lots of other people are doing 'a thing'. Then, it doesn't matter what else the sign says, that 'thing' has become a norm.

The second sign didn't create any kind of norm.

How might you apply this to your fundraising? Well, take the example of a client of mine who wanted to increase the number of regular donors.

They set up a regular donation page. But their page had a twist: they added one of those fundraising totalisers. These don't really work if you have a fundraising target for regular gifts. So what they did instead was use the number of people who had become regular donors.

Last time I looked, their appeal page said at the top: 'Join 3,809 fellow supporters and help us reach our target of 5,000'.

Readers of their page can see there are lots of people giving each month. The progress bar is well over halfway to being complete. This touches a strong drive that's innate to humans, which is to finish things and hit targets.

Hence the classic fundraising thermometer (as used by churches and the beloved UK children's TV show Blue Peter) with only a little bit to go.

My client told me they were doing better than they expected with this appeal.

This is a classic way of showing social proof. The viewer has a feeling that everyone else is doing this thing, and it creates a pressure on them to do the same thing.

Show what's at stake

This is something that the best non-profits do in fundraising. And it works.

You need to spell out what will happen if your reader doesn't give.

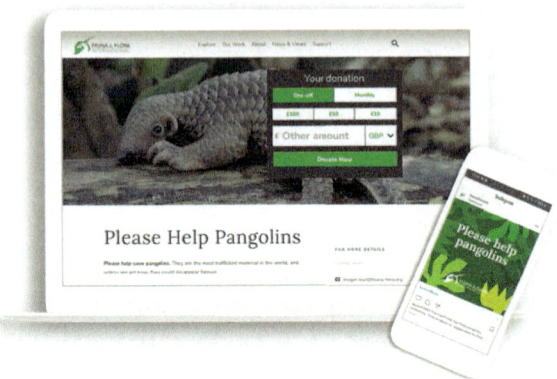

This isn't the best example I could find. But there are lots of things to love about this giving page. Chief among them is the cute pangolin: look at her little face!

Sorry, got side-tracked there…

It's the text we are looking at: 'They are the most trafficked mammal in the world, and unless we act now, they could disappear forever'.

That's what's at stake here; the pangolins could become extinct. That's a compelling reason to give.

Think about what is at stake for the cause you serve. What's the worst-case scenario? Can you show that by giving, someone can help to stop it from transpiring? If you don't have a message about what is at stake, you'll be missing a lot potential giving.

Make this change feel possible

The next thing about giving pages that raise a lot of money (or time) is they talk to one person at a time and that one person is the donor.

The donor is the hero of your story.
You might think your organisation is the hero of the story. You are wrong. Your job here is to connect your donors with the change they want to see.

You are the conduit for your donor, making good stuff happen. And your donor needs to know their donation, no matter how small, will make an impact.

As Jeff Brooks says in his book 'The Fundraiser's Guide to Irresistible Communications'.

'One of the main reasons donors don't give is this: they think their gifts don't matter. My $25 is too small to make a difference. Why bother?'

You need to show this one person that they have power. You need to spell out how their few pounds, or their half hour, will have an effect.

A great example of this is used by another one of my clients, Humanity and Inclusion. This is a part of their giving page:

1. My donation

SINGLE | MONTHLY

£ 5 | £ 8.50 | £ 10

£ Choose your own amount

£5 per month over one year could clear 180m2 of landmines, saving the lives of innocent civilians.
© J. Tusseau/HI

Every gift enables us to make a real difference to the lives of disabled and vulnerable people around the world. Your gift will be used wherever the need is greatest. Thank you.

There are elements of this donation page that make it work well. What I'd like to draw your attention to here is '£5 per month over one year could clear 180 metres squared of landmines, saving the lives of innocent civilians'.

To me the reader, five pounds per month seems doable.

And that £5 clears a huge plot of land. To me at least, that feels like a big space. This is an outstanding example of how a small amount can have a big impact.

Also note that perfect line: 'Your gift will be used wherever the need is greatest'.

All of us, when we write appeals, will face a temptation. I want to steer you away from it because it can spell death to your appeal: using figures that enlarge a problem. I suppose we think, well, if I explain the scale of the problem, people will be more worried about it, and they'll give more.

This approach backfires. The bigger the problem, the more helpless people feel about it and the less likely they are to give.

My friend Jeff Brooks provides examples of this on his website Uncle Maynard's Treasure Trove of Direct Mail Knowledge. This website is like your grandad's attic with all sorts of cool old quirky artifacts in it, but for do-gooders.

All the items on this website were received and kept by an elderly gentleman in the US. He loved to get appeals in the post. That might seem strange to you, but there are loads of people out there who just love to give. And they love reading the stories from non-profits.

You can see exactly how much Uncle Maynard loved to give, because there's a picture on this website of five storage boxes. Each one is full of direct mail this guy had received over his life. He even kept all the envelopes!

Here is one. And this says there are only 22 days left to provide 52,159 meals

Well, they got one thing right. The sense of urgency—22 days left. That's good. But then… then they make a massive 'fail'. They mention 52,159 meals.

My first thought, when I look at this as a donor, is that I want to deny that this is real. It feels too big to solve. I've got 10 pounds to spare; how can I possibly make a dent in that?

I would imagine this appeal didn't do all that well, because of this message on the envelope. And you haven't even opened the letter...

Here's a much better example of an appeal:

This was sent as part of the same campaign.

I wonder if you can tell why this is better?

The answer is that it's showing one child with an empty plate, and it's telling you $1.92 provides a Thanksgiving dinner.

Now that feels doable to me. It's the same campaign, the same charity, and the same season, but now it's a solvable problem. With my 10 pounds, I could feed at least six kids like this lil' guy.

Tell a story

One of the most frustrating things I see is when charities bore their donors to death.

To show you what I mean, have a look at this letter and see how far you can read before your eyes glaze over…

```
Dear Friend,

     HOSPICE and its medical partners, PALLIATIVE CARE, offer per-
sonal, gentle, respectful care and cost-efficient services to people
nearing the end of their lives, and to those who love them. Good
hospice care is always a personal choice, does not shorten or lengthen
life, and is committed to providing the best possible care.

     The last years of the 20th Century were a triumph of successful
medical technology. New surgical techniques, innovative drugs, CAT
scans, MRIs, PET scans, transplants, and the whole gamut of high-tech
equipment and procedures all improved and extended many lives.

     But to all of us will come a time when even the most aggressive
treatment can no longer lengthen life, and then these technologies can
often become a burden rather than a blessing. For those of us lucky
enough to have access to good hospice and palliative care, there is
hope until the very last day of life -- hope for comfort, caring,
pain-free living and support for those we are leaving behind. Sadly,
far too few of us have access to the full range of good hospice care.

     For some, there may simply be no local hospice. In many other
places, only very limited services are available. In other areas,
inexcusably, access to good hospice care is limited because some
doctors refuse to refer patients to hospice care (too often because of
ignorance, prejudice or money). Good hospice care offers care at home,
care in specially designated nursing homes, and increasingly, in
specially designed, purpose-built "hospice houses."
```

I got through barely two sentences. This isn't raising money—it's just boasting. Imagine: a person got paid to write this thing!

I want you to raise money, not stroke your trustees' egos. This is not about you and how brilliant your organisation is (I know that already). It's not about how brainy your staff are, or how long you've been around.

No, no, no.

What you want to do is tell a story like this:

Friday, 10:40 PM

Dear Friend,

    A lady should never get this dirty, she said.

    She stood there with a quiet, proud dignity. She was
<u>incomparably</u> dirty -- her face and hands smeared, her clothes torn and
soiled. The lady was 11.

    My brothers are hungry, she said. The two little boys she
hugged protectively were 8 and 9. They were three of the most
beautiful children I'd ever seen.

    Our parents beat us a lot, she said. We had to leave. The boys
nodded mutely. We had to leave, one of them echoed. The children did
not cry. I struggled to manage part of a smile. It didn't come off
very well. The littlest kid looked back at me, with a quick, dubious
grin. I gave him a surreptitious hug. I was all choked up.

    I would like to take a shower, the lady said.

    Seventeen years ago, I did not know that there were thousands of
runaway, abused and abandoned children like these in this country.

    I learned the hard way.

    One night, in the winter of 1968, six teenage runaways knocked
on the door of my apartment where I was living to serve the poor of
New York's Lower East Side. Their junkie pimp had burned them out of
the abandoned tenement they called "home." They asked if they could
sleep on my floor. I took them in. I didn't have the guts not to.

    Word of mouth traveled fast. (It does among street kids). The
next day four more came. And kids have been coming ever since. it was
these kids -- with no place else to go -- homeless, hungry, lacking
skills, jobs resources -- that compelled me to start Covenant House
over seventeen years ago. <u>Today our crisis centers help tens of
thousands of kids from all over the country-- and save them from a
life of degradation and horror on the streets.</u>

    Kids like the eleven-year-old lady and her very brave little
brothers. They were easy to help: to place in a foster home where
beautiful kids are wanted and loved, and made more beautiful precisely
because they are wanted and loved.

I got through all of that. From the opening sentence it's riveting.
It's focused on three children and it's quite surprising to read.
I'd read more of this story if you gave it to me because I want to
find out the ending to this tale of woe.

There are so many positive things to say about this letter. But
the main point I want to make here is that it tells a story. There's
no boasting or puffery. It focuses on the good that needs to be
done.

Remember who this is really about

Here's another 'what not to do'. The envelope says 'Forty years of helping people grow and their knowledge of God and his holiness'.

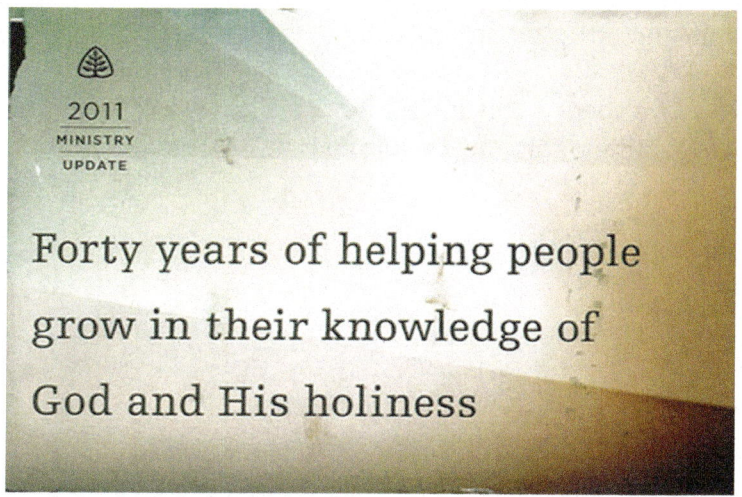

The reason why I'm putting this on the naughty step is it's just talking about the group who sent this. It's all about them. It doesn't mention me, their donor, at all.

My gut reaction is—so what?

Contrast this with the following:

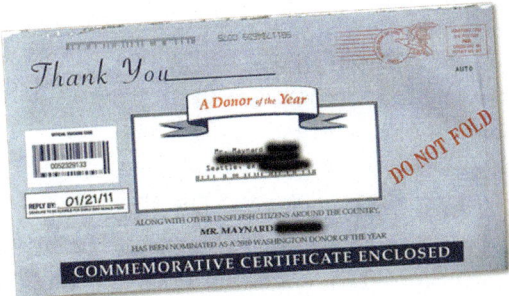

Right on the envelope, above the address, it says 'A Donor of the Year' in a cute little ribbon title.

The text continues: 'Along with other unselfish citizens around the country, Mr. Maynard has been nominated as a 2010 Washington donor of the year'. Then in eye-catching bold colour, it says 'commemorative certificate enclosed'.

This is a bit cheeky because this same mailing would have gone out to thousands of other people just like Uncle Maynard.

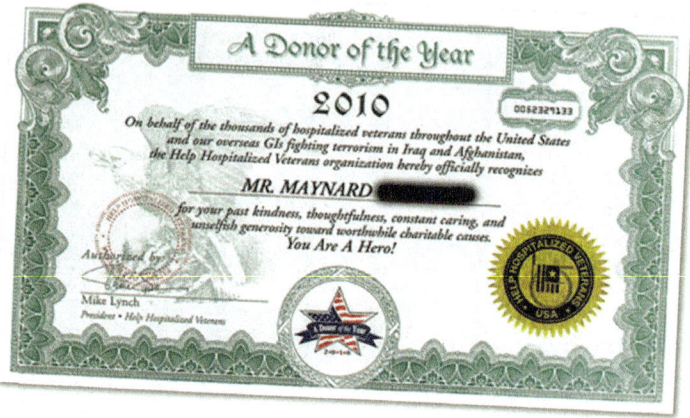

Here's what was inside.

This is a sweet and lovely thing to do for your donor. (Or, well, thousands of people.)

It costs the same as sending out a usual fundraising appeal, but this is all about the person who has been giving the money. It's about recognising their efforts.

Having said all this, you'd need to tweak this, depending on which values group your donors are in. I'll leave you to figure out what tweaks you would need to make this work for Elves and Hobbits.

I bet this would have made Maynard feel really good about himself. It does take kindness, thoughtfulness, constant caring, and unselfish generosity to be a regular donor. And he is indeed a hero.

So, this is one of the best examples I've seen of a focus on the donor.

Now, I'm not saying you should copy this same thing for your donors. You need to know your donors well enough to know what's going to make them feel amazing.

Certainly, a good thank you and news about what their money or time has done—that's going to be common to all values groups.

Because of you

Because of you, we have been able to carry on our caring for Island patients and their families throughout the coronavirus pandemic.

Here are some of the ways your donations are making a real difference to people on the Isle of Wight. Thank you.

Donate now

Still here for care homes   Protected thanks to you   Still making last wishes happen

Here's another way to do this that I found online. This from a hospice in the Isle of Wight.

What I love about this is that they show pictures of the people their donors have helped. And the captions are great, pure, and simple.

It's not going to win any graphic design awards. The photos look amateur, particularly the middle one. Far from being an issue, this lends authenticity. You can tell these are real people. You can tell they really do work for the hospice, and it's clear evidence of what their donors have made happen.

Specific call to action

For your appeal to work, you need a good call to action.

A call to action is the request you make to your donor; the key thing you're asking them for.

This will always go at the end of your appeal and may appear at key points throughout. However, there are good and not so good ways to do this.

Let's see the kind of thing to avoid:

Please give to relieve poverty and suffering around the world, where it's needed most. An incredibly generous group of supporters agreed to double every donation up to a total of £1.5 million and we're thankful to have already met that match funding limit! However, you can still make a huge difference to the lives of people like Mustafa.

I won't mention the name of this non-profit to protect the guilty.

I've taken this from a longer appeal page. There's so much wrong with it.

The first sentence is the call to action. And the first problem is that it's not specific. I have no idea how much cash they want, nor when they want it by. And it's so vague; this could be anywhere in the world, any kind of suffering. So, I can't create a vivid picture in my mind of what my gift will do.

As an aside, it gets even worse. They're now putting me off because I've missed the chance to have my gift doubled. And that was up to £1.5 million. So, now I'm thinking, 'What can my little donation do here?'

Here is a page where the call to action works a little better.

Charity: water don't always get it right, but they do deserve quite a lot of the praise they get for super-stellar fundraising.

Now, I don't agree with everything on this page[16] (if you've been paying attention, you'll see a few things right away). But what is helpful here?

It's this part: 'Your ten pound monthly donation can give four people clean water every year.'

Here is a more ideal example.

This is a quote from Jeff Brooks:

---

16   For example, they say '100% funds water projects.' I don't like this at all. I think it does harm to draw donors' attention to how much of their money is spent on admin. Because admin keeps charities alive; it stops corruption and waste of funds, helps donors and even stops staff getting arrested or fined. People should know how important it is they give to make the admin happen.

Making that the centrepiece of an appeal would bore everyone silly and embarrass the admin staff. But it's the sort of thing you can drip feed to your donors—praise your office manager here, have a 'behind the scenes' there.

'A real call to action leaves nothing to the imagination. For example, your gift of $25 or more sent by December the 31st, will give low-income kids in our community soccer uniforms, so they can compete joyfully in this character-building sport'.

That's specific. It's timely. It tells me what my gift can do in very concrete terms.

That's the ideal call to action. I wish there were more good examples of great calls to action out there.

Design elements

Now let's look at elements of design that create a compelling donation page.

I've taken a screenshot from a website where they show you the innards of tests they've done with non-profit websites.

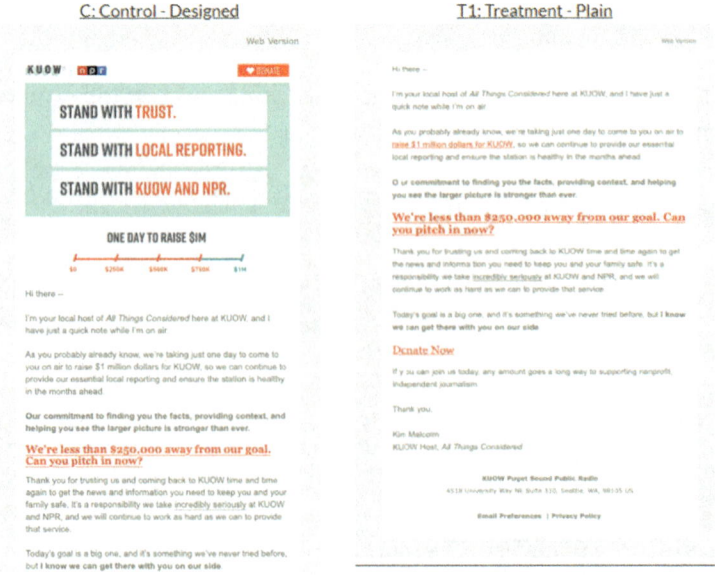

Look at these two treatments of a giving email. These were spilt tested to the same audience.

As a nerd, I love to see if I can guess which test raised more money.

What you're looking at here are emails that were part of a split test. We have the graphic designer's favoured version on the left. One the right, we've got the bare bones text version.

So, stop reading and decide which one you think had a better response. The answer is on the next page.

Did you make your guess?

The results were that the control email design (the one on the left) had a conversion rate of 0.41%. (I know that seems really low, but bear with me. That relates to the number of people who gave, out of all the folks who received this email.) And the test version, the one on the right, got 0.53%.

So the plain text version was the winner.

At first glance, there seems to be a wafer-thin split between these two numbers. Keep in mind these are absolute percentages or percentage points.

If we look at relative percentages, the winner raised 28% more.

You might remember a similar test I ran for a client that doubled their income from email.

This is surprising for a lot of people, particularly designers. That includes me. I studied graphics at art college and made a living that way for a few years.

It was hard for me to hear that the things I'd been taught were harming my clients. Seeing hard evidence that something so ugly worked much better for fundraising—annoying isn't quite the word. Soul destroying would be going too far. I think my feelings were somewhere between the two.

Most designers learn how to craft layouts and imagery that sell products.

I like fashion brands, like People Tree and AllSaints. I'm used to getting gorgeous emails sent to me with pictures of the clothes that are so good you want to eat them. Or surprising design elements that interrupt my normal thought patterns. That works well when you want to sell clothes, but we are not selling clothes.

It does not work for fundraising. Getting people to give is all about the relationship between you and another human being. So, with this test here, **it looks like they're spending their money on the cause rather than on design**.

It looks like an email from a friend. And that's what gets results in the world of fundraising.

Things that look over-designed and slick can repel donors. Showing just who you are and what you do, without pretence: that's what most people long for from a non-profit. Materials that have a swish design can look inauthentic to a non-profit.

There are always exceptions: you would expect the Royal Opera House to be exquisite in everything. But that's part of their cause.

For most non-profits, playing from the heart, looking 'dashed off in a hurry' adds to a sense of urgency.

I also want to point something out about designing a good appeal. Part of this work is making sure that if someone skim reads your stuff, they still take in the key points. That's why NPR enlarged part of the text, made it red and underlined it. 'If you only read one charity sentence this summer…'

It's a link, but it's also underlined because this is the most crucial thing they want you to know.

When you're writing an appeal you want to think to yourself— what three things would I want a donor to know once they finish reading this? Then highlight those sentences.

Images

This is a major part of fundraising: your choice of images.

No image at all is better than a bad image. So, you don't always have to have an image to make your appeal work.

And this, I am afraid to say, is a bad image. This is from an email that was sent to me by an organisation I give to.

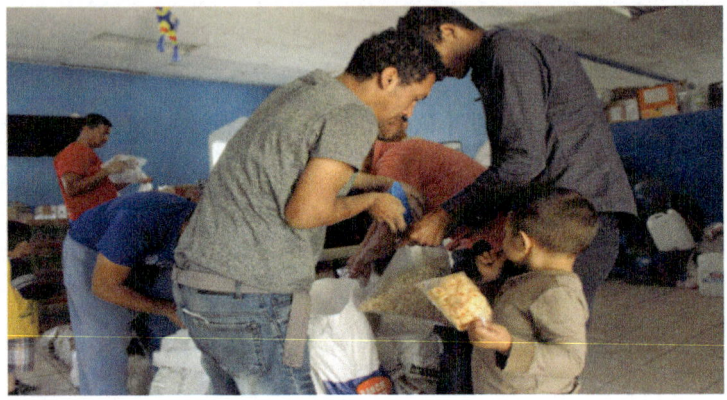

Shelter families sharing food with one another.

There are some things about this organisation that are the best in fundraising I've ever seen. But this is a recent fail that made me shake my head.

I'm confused about what I'm looking at. It's so chaotic they have to use a caption to tell me what's going on.

Worse, everybody's looking away from me. Apart from one guy further to the back, who's partly obscured. He might be looking at the camera, but it's a bit fuzzy so I'm unsure.

Then there's two cute little kids whose faces I can't see. The one in the foreground is holding some junky looking crisp things. Are they hula hoops? Not exactly full of vitamins.

And whatever is in the bag that the two gentlemen are holding looks like bird food.

There's a pile of nonsense in the background. What's that guy on the left doing with his hand in a plastic bag?

There is, as they say, so much to unpack here.

Yes, it's an amateur photo and it's clear to me that it's authentic. But it could have done so much better if this child was looking at the camera. That one small change could take this from a mess to a worthwhile image.

Captions are always worth adding. Of all the things on a page, captions are read the most. But this caption *needs to be there* for me to understand what's going on in the photo.

Yes. They've got food. They're sharing it. That's what they tell us. I'm thinking: 'so what?'

Contrast the previous photo with this one:

There's one subject. I know what I'm looking at. I can see he's trying his best to put on a brave face, but he's not a happy boy.

It looks like either he's got a cold or he's been crying. He's got a hat with a hole in it. He's clutching his guardian's finger. He's just a little bit dirty. My gaze keeps going back to his eyes. This image has woken up my mothering instinct.

Also, it's not poverty porn. There's a dignity to it. But you can see what the need is.

This photo shows that you don't have to use a professional photographer to get this right. In this instance, the lighting doesn't quite work. Part of his face is in shadow, and the sun's hitting another part of it.

It may be a bit posed, but still it's in situ; it's off the cuff.

You don't need a degree in photography to take good fundraising shots. You just have to take images where the need is clear, the subject is making eye contact and the image makes sense.

Also, remember that photo of the scientist earlier on in the book. That smiling guy contradicted the message that time is running out to save lives. Yes, it's great to show a scientist enjoying their work, but it jars with the idea of people being told they have cancer.

If you've read through this chapter, nodding your head and thinking 'but we already do all of that', there's one more aspect that you need to consider for best results.

That is to use digital for something it does best – and that is to tailor each ask to the person who receives it.

If you're at this advanced level and want to learn more about that, thanks to the folks at more onion, here's a free report:

https://whisper.ist/data-integration

Now we've looked at what makes a great appeal, let's have a look at how you can tell your supporters and previous donors about it.

Key Learning Points from this Chapter

There are factors common to all values groups when it comes to persuading your donor to give. These are the ones with the most power:

- A sense of scarcity or urgency.
- Social proof—others are doing this same thing.
- It's clear what is at stake.
- Solving the problem seems within supporters' reach.
- There's a story.
- The appeal focuses on the donor, not the organisation.
- There's a specific call to action.
- The design is simple and looks like it was made by a friend.
- Images make sense, feature a subject who is looking at the camera, and show the need.

Chapter 12:
How to write a great email campaign

Email is by far the best tool for telling your supporters or donors about your need for time or money. Unlike social media, there's no giant corporation who are the gatekeeper for all emails. You can move from one email service to another. Most people who give to non-profits check their email at least once a week. And it's cheap to send; much cheaper than post.

Let's look at how to set things up so your email is more likely to be opened.

Increasing the open rate is one of the best things you can do to increase your online income. This is because it doesn't take a lot of effort to make positive changes.

Once you know the secrets to growing your open rate, you can just keep repeating them. And it's a mere 10 minutes a week of your time.

What I'm about to show you has an outsize effect on how many people open your email and following from that, how many people will give.

There are four components to getting a high open rate, in order of importance:

1. Sender name
2. Previous good experience of reading an email from this sender
3. Timing
4. Subject line

Unexpected, isn't it? Everybody focuses on the subject line because it's easiest to measure the success of. But it's the least important part of getting your emails opened.

Let's look at these one by one.

Optimise your sender name

If you have a well-respected, recognised brand, it doesn't matter so much who the email is from because people know your name. This is only going to be true in a handful of cases, though, like Greenpeace or Save the Children.

Being a smaller player, you rely on subscribers developing a personal relationship with the sender.

This works best if the sender has a strong character — a unique voice — and your supporters get to know that person. If an email comes from a new person (or new to your list, at least) you will see the open rate drop. If you must do this, introduce the new person first. Ensure that as many subscribers as possible see that handover. You could do this by introducing them a few times in different ways over the course of a few emails.

The only exception to this rule is if the sender of a one-off email is famous or already well-known to subscribers. Then you may well see a maintained or increased open rate.

One of my clients sees much success because they put their CEO's name as the sender, and it's signed off by her. People reply, thinking it was she herself who pressed the send button on the email.

Best practice for sender name looks like this:

Rachel, Donor Whisperer

Rachel Collinson (Donor Whisperer)

Rachel C; Donor Whisperer

Or, some combination thereof. You might want to run a split test and see which works best for your list.

If you want to make this even more powerful, introduce your email sender at the moment somebody signs up to your emails. You can use the thank you page to do this. Show their photo and a little bit about them.

This mirrors the process of meeting somebody in real life and exchanging business cards or phone numbers. Anything else is less personal and doesn't fit in so well with natural human behaviour.

What is most vital here is if you're sending from a human being, it needs to be the same person every week.

So, if the people on your list come to know you and like you, they're way more likely to give. If they see your name in their email inbox every week, then they'll start to relate to you as a friend. This makes it harder to break off that relationship.

Previous good experience of that sender

Do you remember the story of Pavlov's dogs I mentioned previously?

You want to get into a situation where your supporter has such a great experience opening each of your emails that they want to relive that again and again and again. Such that whenever they see your email arrive in my inbox, they think 'tasty food!' —and salivate. Or click to open the email. (I did accidentally get saliva on my keyboard once; please don't ask why. It's, erm, not best practice.)

What I'm trying to say is that a previous good experience will prime your supporters to look forward to your emails. That's the top factor in getting them opened—to make opening them compulsive and anticipated.

I want your emails to be as good as having a tasty treat. I want your subscribers to actively seek them out. If an email fails to arrive, I want them to miss it and look out for it.

Once you have this working, it covers all sorts of other problems. I'm not saying it's an easy thing to do by any means, but it's where we want to get to.

There are email lists which achieve this.

There's a myth that goes round the charity sector that you can't send more than one email a week. I am on email lists that send me one email a day, and I still look out for them and enjoy them. Because it's like a tasty snack every time I open them.

If people fall in love with your emails, you can send as many as you like.

Send time

How do you feel when you look at this picture?

Does this look familiar?

According to Vogue magazine, there are two types of email user. One who has an inbox that looks like this with almost six-figures-worth of unopened emails. (I can barely look at this, it makes me so anxious.)

Then there's another type of email user, like me. We want to deal with every single email that comes in as soon as we get it.

I like to keep my inbox to zero. If I have more than 20 emails unopened, I start to get palpitations and twitchy fingers. Currently, I've got over 50 and it's driving me to distraction.

But the other type of person, the one with all these unopened emails, they still manage to muddle along in their lives.

It may surprise you to learn there are way more people whose email inbox looks like the one in the picture. Not everyone is as uptight as me, it appears.

Vogue magazine says that the people whose inbox looks like this are more intelligent than people like me. So of course I think they're wrong.

But to get to my main point: what does this mean for you?

It means that timing is the second most important factor in getting your emails opened. For most people with an inbox like this, they'll just scan the most recent 20 or 30 emails that have come in. The rest? Who knows if they'll ever get to those?

So, you want to be in that person's inbox at the very moment they're looking at their email. That may be only once a day, or it may be three times a day. We just don't know.

Keep reading, because I have created a tool for finding out what the best email send time is for your unique email list. More on that later.

For your edification, here are some stats on non-profit emails. These have been gathered from millions of email sends across the world.

Now, you may be reading this and thinking: "but I saw this webinar that said different…"

I bet you have. That's because these figures vary from country to country and year to year. By the time you read this, things may have changed. If you don't have much data for your list right now, it's worth just trying this rule of thumb to start with. But the best data to rely on is your own, for your own list.

Anyway, with that important caveat out of the way, let's have a look at some graphs.

Rather unhelpfully, this chart numbers weekdays one to seven rather than having the names of the days. One is Monday, two is Tuesday, three is Wednesday and so on.

So, you can see how the blue columns represent the number of campaign emails sent on those days, and the red line is the number of opens.

This shows that Friday is the day on which non-profits send most often. And yet the open rate is second lowest on Friday.

I have my suspicions as to why this is: you start Monday thinking about what email you're going to send that week. You work on it, and then you send it to colleagues to ask if it's okay.

Life happens, it gets delayed, and it doesn't get sent out until a frantic last-minute rush on Friday afternoon. Or you've got to get it out before the end of the week because you have to send that week's email.

From this, however, we can see that's the worst thing you can do because the open rate is so bad on Friday.

What surprised me is that it's also appalling on Saturday. Very few non-profit emails get sent out on Sunday, but the open rate is fourth highest. (Look at that little red line flailing about on its own there and remember that.)

We can see how the open rate is highest on Wednesday and that's only the third most popular day for sending out emails.

Now, let's have a look at click rate. The picture changes here. We've got the highest click rate on a Sunday and we've got the second highest click rate on the first day.

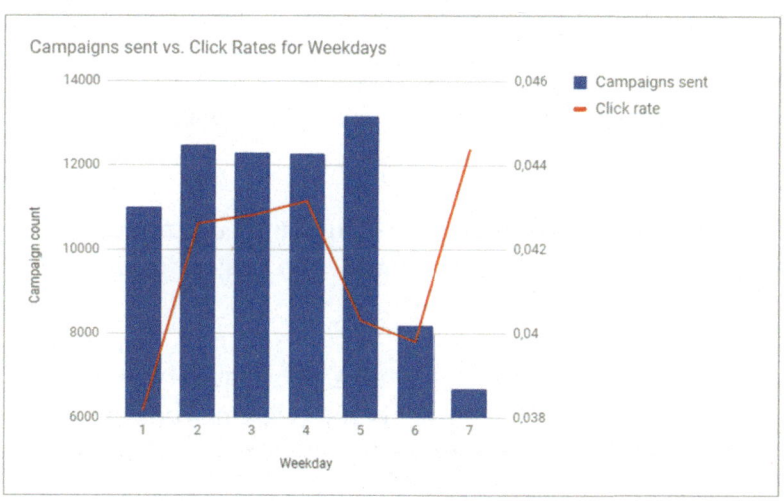

Again, the third lowest click rate is on a Friday. Now, this is average, and this is an example of why best practice doesn't work for everyone. I've tested the time of emails sent for a number of different clients and it does vary from this.

The huge outlier here again is Sunday. Look at that wee red line jutting out to Sunday like a poorly anchored flagpole. So have a look at your own data and see what it tells you.

To recap, send time is more decisive than you think. It will get more serious for most non-profits over the next few years because the volume of email continues to grow and grow.

Generally, Wednesday at lunchtime works best for emails where you're not asking for anything (high open rate). Sunday lunchtime works best for emails where you're making an ask (high click rate). But do test for your own list!

Subject line

Now we come to the gnarly issue of subject lines. Your subject line is the fourth most critical factor in getting your emails opened.

The nice thing here is once you've found the best sender name and the best time to send your emails, the subject line is the only thing you need to change.

When I run my course 'How to write emails that get a response', I show participants a screenshot of my own email box on my mobile phone and ask them which email they would open.

I would have loved to do that here, but I'd need to get permission from all the friends and communities who've sent me emails and that would be a month-long process. Instead, see if you can persuade your partner or family member to let you have a peek at their inbox. We'll have a rule — no touching.

You'll be able to see that in most email programs these days, the software will display the first few words of the email as well as the subject line.

Ask yourself: if this was me, which email would I open first?

You'll see the subject lines which work best will, in general:

- Use emotions (humour and mystery are perfect).
- Ask a question.
- Reference a timeframe or be urgent somehow.
- Pertain to you as an individual.
- Catch your eye.
- Be short.
- Offer something you want.
- Be part of an ongoing conversation.

In all the split tests of subject lines I've done over the years, every single time, short always beats long. (If you do a split test with valid findings that contradicts this, please let me know!)

Short doesn't always beat long in the case of email content, and we'll get onto that soon. But when it comes to sender name and subject line, short always wins over long. You can break most of these rules but if your subject line is short, it's probably still going to work.

Some email programs will give visual emphasis to emails that are part of a back-and-forth, with replies. Gmail adds a number in brackets to show you how many emails are in that thread. This draws the eye even more.

If you only come away from reading this chapter thinking one thing, make it this: 'By gosh, I really need to get people to reply to my emails'.

All the items in the list of what makes a good subject line can be boiled down to one concept: **salience.**

That sums it up.

How relevant will this email be to me and my needs? Is it someone I know? Is it about something I want? Is there a sense of urgency to it?

All these things make the email subject salient. So aim for salience wherever possible.

There is a shortcut to making your emails salient.

You might not have much data on the people in your database. You would need tons of data to create the most salient subject line possible: one that speaks to the things your reader is thinking about at the time. (I would be pretty freaked out if you wrote me an email that helped me choose which Fenech-Soler track I should listen to next.)

You couldn't possibly know that about me; not even my husband would.

But there's one simple trick that means you'll hit the mark more often than not. (And if that sounds like clickbait, let me promise you: it's nothing to do with belly fat.) You use current events and what's in the news.

As I type this, if you were to mention 'Omicron' in your subject line, your open rate would sky-rocket. (I **really** hope that is no longer true by the time you read this.)

The reason this works so well is because repetition creates compulsion. When a person has seen something in the paper, on TV, they've heard it on the radio, and now it's in their email inbox, they're more likely to click on it.

If your subject hasn't been in the news, your email will only get opened if it's super salient to that reader at that moment.

When I come up with ideas for subject lines, I aim for 25 with a minimum of 10. This is hard to do alone, unless you are a 'bonkers ideas person' like me. However, I recommend you brainstorm ideas for subject lines together with your colleagues. (And now you already know a great way of doing that.)

We've taken a thorough look at how to get your email opened; now let's have a look at what text will spur your reader to click through to your appeal.

Repetition

There's a famous line that often gets attributed to Martin Luther King, Jr. Actually, it wasn't him. The earliest instance we know of was in 1908 by the Reverend Fred E Marble. (What a superb name.)

'First I tells 'em what I'm gonna tell 'em, second I tells 'em, and third I tells 'em what I told 'em.'

- Rev Fred E Marble

My dad is a preacher and he's a past master at this. He was the person that first mentioned this quote to me.

You may have heard a similar adage from the advertising world. A person needs to see your message in three different media before they'll trust you enough to buy something or take action.

That's now disputed; most experts think it's a lot more than three times. Of course, it varies from person to person. Human beings are generally slow to trust. This is why brands were invented. But it's also why it's imperative to repeat things.

Humans have evolved to fear new things, which is reasonable. When you think about it —you don't know whether a new thing could kill you.

So, the old parts of your brain, the less evolved bits, are always on the lookout for something out of the ordinary. And your instincts will draw you away from that thing.

Now you know why you hear songs on the radio again and again and again until you're sick of them. (It's why the mere mention of Bryan Adams'"Everything I Do' strikes fear into the hearts of millennials.) That's one of the few ways a song by a new artist gets to number one; if people hear it enough to recognise it.

When it comes to your cause, you'll find it takes a few times for someone to see your cause on Facebook before they'll sign up to your email list. Then it will take them several emails and a few prods of varying kinds to get them to give to you.

There's another theory as to why this works. (And I suspect both are true.)

If you tell a person the same thing in three distinct ways, you have more chances to hit their emotional buttons. As we know, people are not all motivated in the same way.

So, if you're explaining the same thing from one angle, then from another, and yet another, you are much more likely to get a response.

Have you ever got a letter from a non-profit in the post, and that letter is several pages long, and it repeats itself several times? Now you understand why. Their fundraiser knows what they're doing.

You can do this within an individual email (which you should, particularly your call to action) and over the course of the year, too. This is what winning politicians make sure to do with their slogans. 'Take back control' and 'It's the economy, stupid'. None of us will forget them after we've heard, read or seen them for the twentieth time.

Sometimes people ask me, is a short email better than a long one?

My answer is always, the email should be as long you need to put across everything you want to say. When a person is interested in a topic (or they need a reason to procrastinate on cleaning the bathroom) they'll read an awful lot of text. The problem is most emails just aren't that interesting, which has led to the myth that emails need to be short.

If you learn to write well, you can write a long email. And your reader will still drink in every word of it.

There's one more instance where I'm keen for you to repeat yourself. It's your call to action. Try putting this in your email as a button, perhaps a text link or a YouTube video screenshot. This is so that, if a person has read far enough through your email to be convinced, they don't have to scroll far to take action.

When it comes to taking action, great emails are just the starting point. When your reader clicks on the call to action, you need to ensure the experience is slick and consistent. For example – the page where the reader lands makes sense as part of their journey. My friends at more onion have created free guides that show you how to create tests that improve your landing pages:

https://whisper.ist/testing

Simple structure with one topic

Our sector has swallowed the myth that sending a monthly newsletter is 'how it's done'. Such a monthly newsletter is sometimes scrappy and amateur looking, and there's nothing wrong with that at all.

Sometimes, it's beautifully designed like a magazine layout with photos, different articles, links to this and that. Does this sound familiar?

Yet again I'm going to remind you of the test I did with my client in chapter two. That one change, from monthly multi-subject emails to once weekly, single-subject emails that doubled my client's income. Yes, that.

I've tested this lots of times and I've never, ever, even once seen the monthly newsletter beat the single-topic weekly email.

Aside from having one focus, another good reason to keep your emails simple is that simple emails grow your list. Why? They're easy to forward.

Let's say I've got a complex newsletter in front of me. There are boxes and columns and pull-out quotes and sections and different text and images everywhere. I read something in it that I want to forward to a friend.

What do I do? Maybe I struggle to copy and paste the right bit into a new email. I only want to draw their attention to one bit.

But the formatting gets jumbled up. After a minute or so of this, I'll give up. I can't be bothered to type out 'ignore all the other stuff, just look at the bit in the bottom right corner with the picture of the tiny frog' so I just leave it.

You've thus missed the chance to grow your list for free! People seeing a forward from your list and deciding to sign up themselves: that's one of the most effective ways your list will grow.

This brings us to the question of what to put in these emails.

Story

Frank T McAndrew is a fascinating guy. He's professor of psychology at Knox College in Illinois.

His life's work is to explain why stories are pivotal to human culture. He tells us that in the history of the evolution of the human species, people who were fascinated with the lives of others had a greater chance of survival. Those who were not interested in hearing stories about others tended to die off without bringing up children.

Stories are the social currency of human beings.
We don't share statistics around the campfire, do we?

(Maybe some stats nerds do, but I expect they're scared of bonfires due to the safety statistics.)

Remember, if you want your supporters to remember your emails and take action, you need to tell a story. There's no way around it.

Very few people take action in response to statistics. Among them are grant funding organisations. They live and breathe more objective measurements and statistics. But the problem with institutional funders, as we've seen, is that it's hard to get unrestricted income from them.

Back to stories; this is why TV soaps are fantastically popular. Why EastEnders is one of the most-watched programs in the UK and has been for more than 30 years.

If you come to enjoy writing stories, then you'll have huge success with fundraising and campaigning.

Understand the importance of mobile devices

Now, a big change of topic, but one that's vital when it comes to the contents of your emails. This does vary from list to list, but bear in mind that most people will read your emails on a mobile phone.

This is a problem because when you write your email, you do so on a computer with a larger screen. And so it can be hard to relate to what your email will look like on a mobile phone.

There's a simple solution: send your email to your own mobile phone and see if it looks OK.

You can also use a tool like Litmus or Email on Acid. These help you to see what your email looks like in a blinding array of devices of all sizes and makes. You get every possible mobile phone you could think of. This includes Blackberry, which seems weird, but there are lots of people still using Blackberries in developing countries.

It's worth testing on the devices you think your supporters are currently using.

This is yet another reason to stick to the simple structure and format and design I mentioned before. (Are you sick of hearing this yet? There's a reason I keep banging on about it.) If you do, it's so much easier to get your email to work on all email systems, tablets and mobile phones.

A huge pitfall is to spend money on a designer and a technical person to make your emails look gorge. It almost never works on all the devices.

Key Learning Points from this Chapter

Learning to write a good email campaign is one of the best things you can do to grow your unrestricted income. Email is cheap and it's not under the control of one single company.

To maximise responses from your emails:

- Optimise your sender name and use the same one for each email.
- Aim to write emails that give your readers such a good experience each time they open them, that they actively look forward to hearing from you.
- Work out the best time to send emails to your list.
- Write salient, short subject lines to grab attention.
- Use a simple structure with a basic design, one topic and one ask.
- Use repetition, because people absorb information in diverse ways, and they should not need to scroll to see your call-to-action.
- Tell stories, don't use statistics.
- Did I mention sending emails with one topic and one ask?
- Make sure you know what your email looks like on a mobile device, as that's where most people will read it.

Chapter 13:
Building forever loyalty

I've run email training for hundreds of people in non-profits now. There's always a battle around who gets to email who, and how often. If you have that same battle, you're not alone.

It's sad, really, because in most places the wrong decision gets made. (Please pause for a second and picture me clutching fistfuls of hair in frustration.)

This is because most heads of Individual Giving only have experience with what works for direct mail. So, understandably, they make decisions based on that.

This is a bit like a TV advertiser making decisions on telephone fundraising scripts based on what works in TV adverts. You can imagine how well that is going to go.

Email is a different medium to direct mail. It's even more intimate and personal but crowded with more distractions.

I'm going to say it once again—in every test I've done, more regular single-topic emails raise **twice to ten times** as much as a single monthly or quarterly e-newsletter. I see non-profits leave so much cash on the table because of this mistake.

Some savvy fundraisers have got this right because they understand the value of stewardship. That is to say, you need to give back more to your supporters than you ask of them.

The other thing people ask me is: 'Won't we get complaints that we're sending too much email?'

There are two things to say in answer to this. When somebody tells you 'I'm getting too many emails', what they really mean is 'I'm getting too many **boring** emails'.

There are some frequent emails that all of us read compulsively.

For example, if your mum sends you an email twice a week, you would read those emails twice a week—unless your mum is awful. (In which case, I'm sorry and let's try to forget I mentioned her.)

So, any emails that are interesting, useful, entertaining or leave you feeling amazing, are always lovely to receive, no matter how often.

The most dreaded type of email, one nobody ever wants to receive, even once a year, is an email that causes them to feel guilty. This is where non-profits generate most of these complaints: when they harangue their donors. With every single email they ask you for more and more.

As I've mentioned before, don't be 'that friend'.

The answer to this problem is to use what the sector calls a stewardship ratio. The lowest one you can use is a stewardship ratio of one to three.

What it means is for every email you send out containing a hard ask[17] you want to send out three emails that are not an ask for anything, or for something easy

---

17   By 'hard ask', I mean a request for money or for a lot of someone's time or something where they would feel guilty if they said no.

So, your three non-ask emails could be petitions, polls, great stories, thanks, anecdotes, listicles, help guides, and so on. Certainly, at least one or two things that are not asking for anything and are just designed to bring good feelings.

Now, I have heard of non-profits that have a stewardship ratio of one to nine or even greater. So, for every hard ask they make of their supporters, they send nine other emails. Nine thank you's or season's greetings cards or lovely stories and so forth. Those charities astound me with how much money they raise.

So, the higher you can get your stewardship ratio, the better. But if you're just getting started, aim for a ratio of 1:3.

There is just one exception to this rule, which is sending out reminders. So, if you do send an appeal email, then always, always follow it up two or three days later with a reminder.

The reminder should go to people who have neither opened nor clicked on your fundraising appeal email. Just to give them another nudge.

The reason I say two to three days later, is that this ensures your reminder doesn't go out on the same day of the week. So, if you send the appeal email on a Sunday, then your follow-up will be on a Wednesday. Or if you send it on a Thursday, then the follow-up is at the weekend.

I have seen cases where the reminder does better than the original fundraising email! This happens because people do want to give to you. That's why they're on your list, and they really want to help. But your email might have got to them at a bad time.

Being reminded is useful for such people; they will be grateful to you. (I'm serious.) If they are in a better position to donate, then they are even more likely to do so.

Be bold when sending out reminders. They don't count towards your stewardship ratio.

Lastly, I don't want to see any tumbleweed rolling in the gaps between communications. This is the biggest reason people unsubscribe from email lists; they just forget all the things they've subscribed to.

Remember the inbox that had 93,000 unread messages in it? Imagine that sort of person gets an email from you once a month. You only have to arrive in their inbox at the wrong time twice, and they won't have seen anything from you for three whole months. That's enough time for a human to forget they were ever involved with you.

(Sorry, I know that's not what you want to hear, but it happens. I get random emails from non-profits I've no memory of joining, but I'm sure I must have.)

It's harsh, but true: you're not the centre of everyone's world. It's easy to forget when you love the organisation you work for and think about your cause all the time.

For your supporters, you're a smaller part of their whole, much bigger, life.

Now and then my newer clients will get stroppy emails from people. These will say, 'Stop sending me spam! I never subscribed to this!' And my clients look in their database and they can see exactly when that person subscribed. The brittle hot-head has just forgotten they signed up because they haven't seen the emails coming in for a while. And that is the curse of the monthly newsletter...

Research shows us that email lists with one send a month have a far higher unsubscribe rate than lists with more, and this is why.

If you're still worried about sending 'too much email', I have a tip for you—change your unsubscribe link. Make it so if a reader wants to unsubscribe and they click that link, they see a page that says something like:

'I'm sorry to hear you want to leave. Would you prefer to just get fewer emails from us?'

Then you offer them a subscription to a 'once-a-month' email list.

Now that may be too much work for folks on your list who may well leave anyway.

But for some larger non-profits, it's a good way to give people the opportunity to step up or down their level of involvement with you.

Try this: run a split test of the monthly newsletter against the single-topic weekly email. If your newsletter beats the weekly email, I'll buy you your favourite drink of choice. But you must send me your results in full, and they have to be statistically significant.

I deeply love being proved wrong, but here I'm not holding my breath.

Now let me just dismount from my hobby horse and move on to another key component of good stewardship. This is to tell good news stories regularly.

The first place to go for those is your beneficiaries, but you can get good news stories from lots of surprising places. Like your:

- Patrons
- Trustees
- Volunteers

- Donors
- Campaigners
- Stakeholders
- Funders
- Celebrity supporters
- Staff

All of these people will have a good news story to tell about your work.

I want you to be like a magpie, looking for shiny silver good news stories to line your emails with. Who doesn't like good news in this age of nauseating doom-scrolling and unfolding apocalypse?

We've already seen how it benefits you to garner replies to your emails. But the benefits of dialogue go beyond just getting out of the promotions folder or the spam filter.

If you can make your relationship with your supporter a dialogue rather than a monologue—the closer you get to building a kind of deep friendship. That's the foundation of long-term loyalty.

To this end, the more you can learn about your subscribers and donors the better. This is why the supporter survey I talk about is so important. Why not build one into an email sequence that gets triggered when somebody joins your list?

Your first email could have a poll in it. This should be simple to click, and have, at most, three options to choose from. (You can always run another short survey later on in the welcome sequence if you want to learn more).

One of my clients sends out more of these than any other type of emails. They have a huge list, close to a million now, I think. They still see open rates of greater than 50% with stratospheric click rates on these little polls.

One caveat: only ask for data that you have a definite plan to make use of. It's easy to fall foul of data protection regulations by asking for stuff you wouldn't end up using. This is, as far as I can tell, illegal in many countries in the world. (However, I Am Not A Lawyer. Always ask one if you're not sure about your national data regulation laws such as GDPR.)

There are all sorts of creative things you can put in your emails that will build your stewardship ratio. It's time to have fun! As an example, one health charity used creative ideas like a comic book and a recipe quiz. The quiz asked readers to guess which country each recipe was from. (The recipes came from torture survivors helped by this charity.) They built these using the Impact Stack fundraising toolkit, and made sure to only ask for gifts once they had sent 3 emails without a hard ask.

Let me give you another example of how taking care to build forever loyalty can reap rewards. One development charity developed an email journey to engage new sign-ups with the refugee crisis. Part of the email journey explained the tough decisions refugees have to make. It took readers to a landing page where a story unfolded:

"A bomb has fallen near the refugees' home. They have to leave - right now. What do they grab as they leave their home behind?"

In a follow up email users were told stories of real refugees who made this decision. This linked to a blog post that explained what they took and why.

Storytelling like this was mixed with other non-ask emails like case studies and surveys. These emails connected with supporters in a deep way, being personal and designed to evoke strong feelings. This made readers much more likely to become donors at later steps in the journey. The journey changed in response to the user's actions (or lack of). This was done on auto-pilot using Impact Stack together with their chosen email platform.

With these kind of great supporter journeys – among other tactics – the charity recruited over 1000 new donors using Impact Stack.

To cement this friendship and keep your donors around long-term, after someone has donated to you, show them the fruits of their generosity, quick as you can. A tangible result, with proof.

The more you:

- fulfil the donor's hunger to satisfy their values,
- delight them with good news stories,
- build a dialogue with them…

…the longer they'll stay with you and give to you loyally, perhaps in increasing amounts. Or persuade their employer to make you the cause of the year. Or even, at the end of their life, they might leave a large portion of their estate as a gift to you in their will.

Key Learning Points from this Chapter

Once somebody has given to you, it's crucial you continue to build their loyalty. This will secure their second, third and umpteenth gifts. The more you cement that loyalty, the longer they will walk alongside you.

To do this, you need to understand what a stewardship ratio is and how to use it in your email communications plan. Aim for a ratio of 1 to 3, where 1 is an email with a hard ask and 3 are emails with soft asks or no ask at all. Reminder emails for appeals are the only exception to this.

Loyalty is built by regular exchanges—once a week or more. Think of it as friends having a lovely correspondence. Tumbleweed gaps between correspondence will kill your list quicker than a data breach.

Most of all, send good news stories whenever you can, especially ones that update the donor on the good their money or time has created.

Chapter 14:
Some advice on the tech you need for this

One of the questions people like you ask most often is about the tech needed to make all of this happen. I've resisted writing about it, because I think that the tech is the easy bit compared to everything else. (Yes, really! Messy people stuff; finding and telling good stories; those are the tricky bits that most people leave too little energy for. Which is why most of this book is about the messy people stuff.)

There's more: every cause's needs are different. There is no one perfect widget that works for all causes. So if you hear any kind of guru type person say 'here's the exact thing you need, go for it', run. Run for the hills! They are leading you astray.

I've started as I mean to go on by suggesting all sorts of tools you can use to build your 'Irresistible Lure'.

However, people still ask how to put everything together. So here I am, answering. Hey, I'm a people pleaser; what can I say?

There are five basic components you need to make all of this work:

- Sign-up tool (like Impact Stack or Engaging Networks) This is the bit of the tech that allows you to create your 'Irresistible Lure' and receive the all-important name and contact details of your potential donor

- Database / Constituent Relationship Management System (CRM) (like Salesforce, Beacon CRM or Donorfy)
  Once you've got the contact details, you need somewhere to put them - and we call this a CRM.

- Mass emailer (like Campaign Monitor, MailerLite or DotMailer)
  This enables you to send emails that are personalised to each person in your CRM.

- Donation platform (like Impact Stack or JustGiving)
  A good donation platform allows you to create compelling donation pages just like the ones we looked at earlier. It will allow you to accept single donations or recurring ones (like monthly membership payments, for example).

- Tracking and analytics (like Funnelll or Google Analytics)
  You'll need a way to measure how well you're doing with all of these bits and pieces. Like, what percentage of people put their details into your irresistible lure form once they land on it?

Some non-profit technology companies have platforms that offer you everything all together - Engaging Networks is one that offers a mass emailer, donation platform and sign-up form tool as well as a simple CRM and tracking tool. This is called the "all in one" approach.

Others decide to do one or two things really well, and enable you to connect their bit of the system to others. Impact Stack is an example of that approach. This is called "best of breed" (yes, like Crufts) or "best in class" if you prefer human-centred metaphors.

I've helped charities to set up both options. However, most often, I find that the benefits of the "best in class" approach outweigh the down-sides. The down-sides are that it can be difficult to hook up all these different systems together. It also means that your staff have to learn several different interfaces rather than just one.

However, as I'm sure you're aware (and may grimace at the reminder) tech changes at a rapid pace. So quickly, that even giants like Salesforce and Blackbaud can struggle to keep up with the needs of non-profits.

What I've seen is that providers who focus their energy on one 'module' in this system (such as analytics) tend to:

- Build a larger community of users
- Offer systems that are easier to use
- Add new features more often
- Have more advanced features
- Offer pre-built connections to other systems.

No software can be the best at everything, so it's a good sign when a system doesn't try to offer All The Things. As a result, it stays simple. You don't have an interface crammed with every feature that every customer might need.

Also - and I'm sorry to remind you about this - your organisation will change. (As will you!) We all had strategies and goals before the pandemic in 2019… I bet those goals would make you laugh if you looked back on them now.

As night follows day, your goals will be unrecognisable in the next three years' time. So the tools that you need to achieve those goals will also change. With a "best in class" approach, it's easier to change. You can swap out one part or another within the system, rather than having to change the entire thing.

This also means you can get going quicker. If you're just changing one part of the system, training and implementation takes less time. You can spend more time finding new donors and less time being annoyed by your procurement process.

Many organisations choose niche tools, and stick them all together like lego parts. A good reason for doing this, rather than using an "all in one" system, is simple: tech changes all the time as well. When you realise one part of your system no longer fits your needs, you can replace just that part. You don't need to go through the hassle of changing everything just for one bit.

Changing all systems at once is a lot of work, costly and therefore often a barrier.

While a lot of good causes have similar needs, they are not the same. A "one size fits all" software firm will have to compromise at some point.

By adopting a "best in class" approach, you can choose the tools that fit your needs best. Do you care more about how easy it is to create and send an email than you do about every detail of its impact? If you do, what CRM will the email tool go well with?

Or, you might have some tools in place that you're happy with, and you don't want to be forced to change those. If you already have an email marketing tool that serves you well, for example, you can plug in the missing part.

One of the "best in class" systems I often recommend is Impact Stack.

They take the approach an "integration first" approach. This is techbro speak for a company that don't try to sneak their digital tentacles into every bit of your organisation's function. Instead, they offer to connect to the tools you already use, meaning you can work in a seamless way with different systems at the same time.

For example, a large UK charity combating homelessness uses Impact Stack's API. (This is like of set of plug sockets which allow pieces of software to connect to each other.) This means they can pull out any supporter data in almost real-time.

From a central place within the organisation, it sends this supporter data to other applications, such as their CRM, and their email marketing tool. Through these, the organisation can pick the best system for each specific use case: the best CRM, the best email marketing tool, and the best platform for digital mobilisation and donation pages.

Impact Stack are kindly offering any reader of this book a free demo. To take advantage of that, go here:

https://whisper.ist/impactstackdemo

For many smaller and mid-sized charities who are forging ahead with individual giving as an income stream, using a complex fundraising database or Customer Relationship Management (CRM) system is not feasible. The cost is too high and the board may not sign off the extra investment in the infrastructure until they can see it proving its worth.

If that's where you are, a system such as Impact Stack or Action Network can do a similar job to a CRM. Either system can handle simpler tasks, like acting as a hub to collect donor data and staying in touch with your supporters.

One of my clients, an organisation with a large supporter base all over the world, started using Impact Stack for fundraising as well as online actions. They managed to build a database of 35,000 contacts from scratch. This also generated 473 one-off donors and 25 regular givers within a year.

Organisations with more mature tech in place will already have a CRM system or fundraising database. For these organisations, it's central to ensure every other system integrates well with the CRM.

Conclusion

Chapter 15:
What to do next

We've reached the end of our time together so far, lovely change-maker. It's my burning desire and hope that you, your staff and the cause you serve have already seen benefits as a result of reading this book.

To recap:

1. At the start of this book, we had a look at the status of your non-profit. We examined the hurdles you needed to clear to get where you want to go. This is so you can pay your staff what they are worth, and make even bigger changes in the world for good.

I made some prescriptions for you based on the results of your assessments.

You should now have a clear vision in your mind of what changes you can make to turn things around. You should understand how the Values-Driven Fundraising System may well be the key to solving your problems.

2. Next, we looked at all the ways in which the Values-Driven Fundraising System could serve to grow your unrestricted income. We considered the challenges that come with mass individual giving campaigns.
3. In the next section of the book, we went through each step in the system, exploring the reliable science behind it.

We had a whistle-stop tour of:

- The donor discovery system.
- The MoVA formula.
- Secret lightning appeal tests;
- Building an irresistible lure.
- Wooing future donors.
- Crafting compelling appeals.
- Building forever loyalty.

4. Finally, we looked in detail at how you can:

- Get to know your best donors and test those findings scientifically.
- Build a sign-up mechanism that will work, while you sleep, to grow your list of individual donors, day in, day out.
- Write compelling appeals that push your best donors' buttons according to their values and motivations.
- Ensure your donors walk alongside you for the rest of their lives.

By the end, we uncovered the parts of the Values-Driven Fundraising System that will make the biggest shifts in your unrestricted income, most quickly.

You should now have a strong understanding of what you need to do to unlock the Giving Code, kick your fundraising up a gear, keep your talented staff and even hire more.

The next step for you is simple:

Get started.

Decide if you need help or if you want to go it alone, but start.

Throughout this book there are all sorts of small changes you can make. Any one of these shifts could take just hours and bring in thousands of pounds more for you each year, as my clients have shown, time and again.

Your income grows one single donor at a time. This book won't turn you into Oxfam overnight, but it can bring you millions in revenue over your organisation's lifetime.

You start this journey with a single first step.

If you decide you'd like help, reach out to me here and let's have a chat:

http://whisper.ist/breakthrough

The small Donor Whisperer team have worked with all sorts of causes from giant nine-figure behemoths to tiny start-ups who've raised only a few quid. Over the last twenty years we've seen and fixed all sorts of problems.

There's just one thing you need to be able to do before you call me. Make sure you can prove that you and your team really do make this planet a better place in some way (however small). If that's you, we want to show you how to multiply that power so you can do even more good in even more more places.

Here's to building a lovelier world together,

Rachel

Chapter 16:
How to get help

Here, I'm going to include a few extra resources for you to access as a reader of this work.

I'm going to be transparent about my reasons for giving you even more useful stuff. Partly, it's about rewarding persistence (well done for getting to the end of this book!). Partly, these are tools that make more sense as a spreadsheet or a video rather than in book form.

The links below will take you to privately hosted pages where you can access the tools, whether downloads, videos or other things.

Also, I've included info and a link on how my team and I can help you crack the Giving Code. We have a few different offerings, from DIY programmes to 'Done-For-You' options. Read on for more details on that.

Find the Optimum Time To Send A Fundraising Email

(Or, **OTTSAFE** for short!)

Use this tool to fill in data on the open and click-through rates of your emails. Provided you have enough data (at least five for each day or timeslot) it will tell you which day of the week and which time of day are best for sending either an appeal or a non-ask email.

http://whisper.ist/ottsafe

Get loads more people opening your emails in 20 minutes

This link will take you to a video that shows how to run an email subject line brainstorm with your colleagues. Coming up with 25 possible lines seems hard, but when you use this method, you'll be amazed how easy it is to reach at least ten great choices in a matter of minutes.

http://whisper.ist/subjectlines

Revive a dying list

Are you seeing open rates of 20% or less on your email list? This downloadable pack features full instructions and template emails to use that can help you reactivate 15% or more of the people on your list who've gone quiet.

http://whisper.ist/reactivate

Further resources

My friends at more onion, the digital mobilisation agency, have put together a tonne of resources on many of the practical aspects of this book. These include creating great user journeys, testing and optimising your web forms, and integrating your technology to create smooth and persuasive experiences from email to web page. All those and more are here:

https://whisper.ist/resources2

Work with me and my team to accelerate your results

I'm always on the hunt for the next big client case study! My star students not only grow their individual giving ten times over but they also get speaking invitations to conferences all over the world, new job offers and pay rises.

If you love what you've read in this book and want help to multiply your unrestricted income sooner, please book a call with me and my team here:

http://whisper.ist/breakthrough

If that's you, do it now[18]. Your staff, and the people or animals who need your help, deserve for your income to grow.

---

18 Yes, even if it's 11pm on a Saturday. My time fills up fast.

About the author

Rachel became a donor for the first time at the tender age of 12 after her dad gave her a Greenpeace 'Save the Whale' poster; a pull-out he found in his newspaper. She fell in love with these gentle giants and all their alien peculiarities. At least one week's pocket money went to Greenpeace soon thereafter.

From that point on she dedicated her life to good causes. From sleeping rough for a night (in a cardboard box in the back garden) as a teenager to raise awareness of homelessness, to joining a protest of around a million people against the Iraq war.

Since completing her post-grad degree in 1999, she has worked with non-profits all over the world, from Australia to Brussels and Costa Rica to Dharamsala.

In her spare time, Rachel is an avid board-gamer. She is an adoptive mum to feline fur-babies Cleo and Susie. She loves making mixtapes for friends and visiting her family in Scotland.

Above all, she believes you need to go straight to the root of a problem rather than treating the symptoms. She's always thinking about how to dig deeper down to get at those roots.

All enquiries for podcast appearances, video shows, conferences or articles can be sent to rachel@donorwhisperer.co.uk

Printed in Great Britain
by Amazon